Studies of the New Testament and its world

EDITED BY JOHN RICHES

THE CHARISMATIC LEADER
AND HIS FOLLOWERS

The Charismatic Leader
and His Followers

MARTIN HENGEL

translated by
JAMES GREIG

Wipf & Stock
PUBLISHERS
Eugene, Oregon

Originally published as *Nachfolge und Charisma*

Wipf and Stock Publishers
199 W 8th Ave, Suite 3
Eugene, OR 97401

The Charismatic Leader and His Followers
By Hengel , Martin
Copyright©1968 by Hengel, Martin
ISBN: 1-59752-077-2
Publication date 1/28/2005
Previously published by Walter de Gruyter & Co. , 1968

Dedicated to

my theology teachers in Tübingen

with respect and gratitude

Editor's Foreword

It is a particular pleasure to be able to initiate a series of studies in the New Testament and its world with a work as distinguished as Professor Hengel's *The Charismatic Leader and His Followers*. Not only does it set the highest standards of critical historical scholarship, but in it Hengel applies his scholarship to a topic of central importance both for the understanding of Christian origins and for the criticism and development of Christian doctrine. The concentration on a single aspect of Jesus' teaching and its illumination by comparing and contrasting it with analogous contemporary phenomena yields insights which are of value not only to the student of Jesus' life and teaching but also to the student of the development of Christian ministry and preaching and of the Synoptic tradition. At the same time such historical insights should prove fruitful in the study both of christology and of ecclesiology. The methodological rigour and attention to detail together with the range of implications of this first volume provide an indication of the aims of the series as a whole.

My thanks go both to Dr Geoffrey Green of T. & T. Clark for his enthusiasm and interest in this series, and to Jim Greig whose understanding of the subject and of the German language is well borne out by the clarity and elegance of his rendering.

John Riches

Glasgow, 1980

Contents

Preface

The following study is based on my trial lecture given on January 25th, 1967, before the Protestant Faculty of Theology at the Eberhard-Karls University in Tübingen.

I substantially extended and supplemented it in the weeks that followed but the structure and sequence of thought for the lecture has been deliberately adhered to. The whole is intended to contribute to discussion of the question of the historical Jesus, and in particular to the problem of what is meant by following Jesus and being a disciple of his, for this subject has recently become again a focus of scholarly interest.

My thanks are due to the Protestant Faculty of Theology in the University of Tübingen which facilitated my return to my theological calling by granting me a research assistantship after many years of other activities on my part; also to Professor Dr W. Eltester for his readiness to include the work in the *Beihefte zur Zeitschrift für die neutestamentliche Wissenschaft,* and to the following: my respected teacher, Professor Dr O. Michel for the understanding and patience with which he has followed my professional career in its various phases, and for many valuable discussions; Professor Dr E. Käsemann for his suggestive questions and Professor Dr H. Gese for the additional information he provided. Finally, I wish to thank my friends and colleagues for the suggestions and helpful co-operation which by dint of discussion on our common subject-matter make our scholarship in the field of theology all the more fruitful. I also wish to thank cand. theol. Klaus W. Müller for his help in reading the proofs and for providing the index.

Martin Hengel

Tübingen, September 1967

Introduction

In research on the Gospels in the last few decades, and in enquiry as to the historical Jesus – which has again come to the fore – the problem of what is meant by discipleship and following someone like Jesus has, strangely, taken a back seat. In the bibliography to his article *Jesus Christus*,[1] Conzelmann mentions, apart from two entries in the *Theologisches Wörterbuch*, only E. Schweizer's monograph, *Erniedrigung und Erhöhung bei Jesus und seinen Nachfolgern* (E.T. *Lordship and Discipleship*, 1960) which likewise deals only relatively summarily, on 13 pages,[2] with the question of following Jesus. At the end of 1962 it is true there appeared a comprehensive and thorough Catholic monograph by A. Schulz called *Nachfolgen und Nachahmen* (*Following and Imitating*) in which, on the basis of G. Kittel's and K. H. Rengstorf's terminological studies and of the material collected in Billerbeck,[3] it was emphatically held that Jesus' summons to 'follow after' him was to be understood by analogy with the rabbinical use of language in the expression *halakh 'aḥᵃrê*, taken to mean 'teacher and pupil living together in the service of the Torah.'[4] In our view, however, Schulz has not only read too much into the meaning of the rabbinical phrase, but has also put a largely false construction on following Jesus, which may not be taken as referring to

[1] RGG 3rd ed., 3, 652 on 8 (E.T. *Jesus*, 1973, 33); see also preface by A. Schulz *Nachfolgen und Nachahmen*, StANT 6 (1962) and W. Bieder, *Die Berufung im N.T.*, AThANT 38 (1961) 6. E. Lohse includes some further literature in RGG 3rd ed., 4. 1286-88.

[2] AThANT 28 (1962²), 8-21. From the Catholic point of view see also K. H. Schelkle, *Jüngerschaft und Apostelamt*, 1958, 11-32; cf. the survey in E. Larsson, *Christus als Vorbild*, ASNU 23 (1962), 29-47. The more recent presentations of Jesus in German deal only sparingly with the question. See E. Percy, *Die Botschaft Jesu*, LUA 49, 5 (1953), 168-174: G. Bornkamm, *Jesus von Nazareth* (JvN), 1956, 133-140 (E.T. *Jesus of Nazareth*, 1960, 144-152); O. Betz, *Was wissen wir von Jesus?* 1965, 47-51 (E.T. *What do we know about Jesus*, 1968, 71ff.). Cf. also J. J. Vincent, ThZ 16 (1960), 456-469, who does more to indicate the difficulties than to provide solutions. V.'s article contains a bibliography of the earlier literature. Still valuable today is J. Weiss, *Die Nachfolge Christi und die Predigt der Gegenwart*, 1895, 2-38. The following titles have been announced, but at the time of going to press had not yet appeared: H. D. Betz, *Nachfolge und Nachahmung Jesu Christi im N.T.*, BHTh 37 (1967), and F. Hahn's essay 'Die Nachfolge Jesu in vorösterlicher Zeit' in *Die Anfänge der Kirche im N.T.*, Evang Forum 8 (1967). On H. D. Betz see further pp.84ff.

[3] G. Kittel, art. ἀκολουθεῖν ThW 1.211-215 (E.T., 1.213f.); K. H. Rengstorf, art. διδάσκειν op.cit. 2.142f. (E.T. 2.135ff.) and μαθητής-μανθάνειν op.cit. 4.437f, 447ff. (E.T. 4.390-461). In contrast to Schulz, Rengstorf emphasizes more strongly the difference from the rabbis, see op.cit. 450ff. For rabbinical linguistic usage see also Bill 1.187f., 527ff., and p.52f. below, note 54.

[4] Op.cit. (n.1), 33; cf. also 21, 35, 43f., 53, 55f., 63, 66, 78f. We may take 127 as typical: 'Jesus invests his activity as Messiah with the concrete form of a contemporary Jewish teacher of the Law'.

1

being a pupil by analogy with what happened in the rabbinical schools. C. G. Montefiore, the great Jewish scholar and leader of Reform Judaism in England, gave clear expression to the true facts of the case with reference to Mt 8.21f.: 'Discipleship such as Jesus demanded and inspired (a following, not for *study* but for service – to help the Master in his mission, to carry out his instructions and so on) was apparently a *new thing*, at all events, something which did *not fit in*, or was not on all-fours, with usual Rabbinic customs or with customary Rabbinic phenomena'.[5]

In what follows, some attempt is made – likewise on the basis of Mt 8.21ff// – to examine Montefiore's thesis in detail, and to provide more specific justification for it – both exegetically and in terms of *Religions-geschichte* – against the background of Jesus' activity and of the age in which he lived.

   [5] C. G. Montefiore, Rabbinic Literature and Gospel Teachings, 1930, 218.

1. On the exegesis of Mt 8.21-22: 'Let the dead bury their dead'

The starting point for investigating the problem of 'following' Jesus should be in the detailed individual analysis of all the relevant *pericopae* and logia and this should embrace redaction and form criticism, plus *Religionsgeschichte*.[1] Here, however, we must limit ourselves to the pericope in Mt 8.21f = Lk 9.59f, which has up to now been given little detailed consideration; and we must investigate it as if it were, to an extent, a paradigm for all the others, and so proceed from there to the question of the meaning of Jesus' call to follow him as a whole.

1 Redaction and form criticism

Our passage stands within a larger unit consisting of sayings about 'following' which have come from the Q tradition. This unit comprises three pericopae in Luke and two in Matthew (Lk 9.57f. = Mt 8.19f.: the saying about the homelessness of the Son of man, then our saying about burying the dead, and finally, in Lk 9.61f., the saying about the man at the plough). While Luke skilfully inserts these sayings directly into the context of the departure for Jerusalem and the second mission (of the seventy-two),[2] Matthew provides a psychological basis for them through Jesus' journey to the other shore of the lake (8.18) and makes the subsequent tale of the stilling of the storm almost symbolically into a prototype of what it is actually to 'follow'.[3] Both evangelists have made certain changes: Matthew makes the questioner a disciple (ἕτερος δὲ τῶν μαθητῶν) and makes the question start with a κύριε, which he mostly reserves for the disciples; even the subject, verse 22a, 'Ιησοῦς, is probably additional (it is lacking in ℵ pc it, cf. sy^s). By way of clarification, Luke places an invitation by Jesus to follow him at the beginning and thus makes the passage into an explicit call-narrative (εἶπεν δὲ πρὸς ἕτερον·

---

[1] Progress in Synoptic research to a great extent depends on such detailed analysis of small units, which in contrast to subjective assessments really do provide evidence and also constructively tackle the literature, which has become completely unamenable to survey. A splendid example of an analysis which thus makes headway is provided by G. Lindeskog, 'Logia-Studien', StTh 4 (1952/53), 129-185 on the detached saying in Mt 13.12// Cf.186: 'Each logion requires just as thorough an examination as the one first dealt with'.

[2] Lk 9.51; 10.1; the VL '72' is without question to be preferred (as in p^75 BD pc lat sy^sc).

[3] G. Bornkamm, WuD NF 1 (1948), 45-53 and in G. Bornkamm, G. Barth, H. J. Held, *Überlieferung u. Auslegung im Matthäusevangelium*, 1965 4th ed., 49-54 (E.T. *Tradition and Interpretation in Matthew*, 1963, 52ff.) cf. also H. J. Held, op.cit. 191f. (E.T. 200ff.).

3

ἀκολούθει μοι) and finally he justifies the brusque rejection of the request at the end by Jesus' commission: σὺ δὲ ἀπελθὼν διάγγελλε τὴν βασιλείαν τοῦ θεοῦ, a formula which is typical of the Lucan work.[4] Taking into account these redactional additions and alterations, the pericope in Q could originally have run as follows: ῞Ετερος δὲ εἶπεν· ἐπίτρεψόν μοι πρῶτον ἀπελθεῖν καὶ (thus Mt; Lk has ἀπελθόντι) θάψαι τὸν πατέρα μου· ὁ δὲ λέγει (thus Mt; Lk has εἶπεν δὲ) αὐτῷ· ἀκολούθει μοι, καὶ (thus Mt: this is lacking in Lk) ἄφες τοὺς νεκροὺς θάψαι τοὺς ἑαυτῶν νεκρούς. On this reading all three pericopae on 'following', which may well have already been linked together in Q, would display exactly the same structure – manifestly a triad in a two-part composition technique:[5] thus the question from an intending but anonymous follower[6] is in each case followed by Jesus' answer, which rejects the expectations of the questioner. In contrast to the call-narratives in Mark (1.16ff. and 2.13f.), which have a different structure, there is lacking any hint as to the place where the action is set, the identity of the follower, and the effect of the logion or the invitation.[7] It is not the presentation of the miraculous

[4] On the redactional treatment see J. Schmid, 'Mt. u. Lc,' BSt 23, 2-4 (1930), 256f., cf. F. Hahn, Christolog. Hoheitstitel, FRLANT 83 (1964²), 83f. (E.T. The Titles of Jesus in Christology, 1969, 80f.). W. Bussmann, Synoptische Studien, 1929, 2, 62 points to the stylistic improvements in Lk. J. Wellhausen, Das Evangelium Lucae, 1904, 47 prefers the introduction in Lk 9.59 and is followed by E. Klostermann, Mt. 1938, 3rd ed., 77; the latter also supposes that Lk 9.57-62 was already combined in Q with the Mission speech in 10.1: Lc. 1929, 2nd ed., 112. But the simpler Matthaean form is probably to be preferred. In the original Q form there was as yet no reflection on how far those who were asking the questions were already disciples or only wanted to be such. It is not their persons but only Jesus' answer which was the focus of interest. On the typically Matthaean addition of κύριε see G. Strecker, Der Weg der Gerechtigkeit, FRLANT 82 (1962), 124. The first questioner, a scribe, addresses Jesus only as διδάσκαλε, possibly the κύριε could also have been taken over by Mt from the Q draft of Lk 9.61, cf. F. Hahn, op.cit.84. But it is more probable that it represents an addition in Lk 9.61. On the other hand omission of the respectful address in Lk 9.57 and 9.59 does not seem very likely. The shortest form is most likely to be identical to the original Q version; cf. below n.11. On Lk 9.60b, see R. Bultmann, Geschichte d. Synoptischen Tradition FRLANT 29 (1931²), 94, 353 (E.T. History of the Synoptic Tradition, 1961, 90, 326). It is 'manifestly a favourite phrase of the author's': E. Bammel, Studia Evangelica III, 2 TU 88 (1964), 8.

[5] See R. Morgenthaler, Die lukanische Geschichtsschreibung, AThANT 14 (1949), I, 74f., who certainly ascribes this scheme of composition to Lk, while in this case it probably goes back to Q – in a fashion to be corrected at vv. 59f. in the light of Mt 8.21f. F. Hahn op.cit. 83 supposes that Lk 9.61f. was a secondary accretion in the pre-Lukan Q tradition and thus was not available to Mt. But it could also be that Mt omitted Lk 9.61f. because it says nothing more than Mt 8.21f. = Lk 9.59f. and was therefore unnecessary in the context of his compactly arranged composition. It was not possible to insert too many intermediate links between Mt 8.18 and 8.23 without disturbing the flow. Cf. also A. Schulz op.cit. (n.1) 105. E. Bammel's groundless ascription of Lk 9.62 to the movement of John the Baptist, is wide of the mark, op.cit (n.9).

[6] The later tradition tended to embroider. In 8.19 Matthew has already turned the first questioner into a scribe, and according to Clem. Alex. Strom. 3.25.3 the questioner in Mt 8.21 was Philip, see Th. Zahn, Das Evangelium des Lukas, 1920, 3rd and 4th eds., n.53.

[7] See the detailed analysis of the Markan call-narratives in A. Schulz op.cit. (n.1), 97-105. Even Mk 3.13-15, which is Mark's own formulation, belongs to this context.

effect of Jesus' call to follow him which matters in the Q pericopae, but the rigorous, categorical element which lies behind this call. Common to Mark and Q is the reduction of the form to a minimum, the lack of any psychological justification – and clear parallels in form and content to the call of Elisha by Elijah, 1 Kings 19.19ff.[8]

Thus even during the period of the oral transmission of the traditions of 'following' two formative components were at work influencing the process: (1) the prototype of the call of a prophet and (2) a hortatory concern, the desire to bring out as clearly as possible the essential nature of Jesus' call and its binding force: with Mark, the ἀκολούθει μοι (Mk 2.14 cf. 1.17,20) acquires in Jesus' mouth a potency which is quite simply miraculous and which abruptly detaches those called from their previous obligations; in Q it is shown that following Jesus plunges the disciples into total lack of security – e.g. in the logion about the homelessness of the Son of man, Mt 8.20// – and requires a break even with the strongest of human links, the family (Mt 8.21f.// and Lk 9.61f.). Thus we can with R. Bultmann speak of 'ideal scenes' in both cases,[9] though Dibelius' term 'paradigm' is, it is true, even more apt:[10] the pericopes on following have a marked 'exemplary' character.

2 What the logion states

However, this formal characterisation still does not answer the question of the historical background. For the saying of Jesus which interests us, ἄφες τοὺς νεκροὺς θάψαι τοὺς ἑαυτῶν νεκρούς, is in fact hardly one that can stem from the tradition either of the Jewish or of the later community. Even as an isolated logion of Jesus it would make little sense without the prior question from the disciple, and the link with the call to follow him. Detached from this context, such a saying could at best be attributed to Cynic polemics directed against inherited taboos and against the expense

[8] See the contrast in op.cit. 100ff. Cf. also below, pp.16ff., n.1-3. On Lk 9.62 see E. Klostermann *Lk*, 1929 2nd ed., 62.

[9] Op.cit. (n.59f. 9) (E.T. 56f.): 'of course, historical reminiscence can be retained in such stories but, in any case the report is stylized. . . .' (60) (E.T. 57). See also A. Schulz op.cit. (n.1) 99, 105. Even if Mk 1.16-20; 2.14 'condenses into one symbolic moment what was in actuality a process' (Bultmann, op.cit. 60) – in which connection we should bear in mind that the 'uniqueness' of the Synoptic call-narratives points back to the 'uniqueness' of the 'process of development' underlying them and no longer capable of reconstruction – that still hardly justifies one, in 'emending' Mk 1.16ff. on the basis of Jn 1.35-49 by psychologizing in the fashion of A. Schulz, op.cit 112ff. or A. Schlatter, *Die Geschichte des Christus*, 1921, 125.

[10] M. Dibelius, *Die Formgeschichte des Evangeliums*, 1933, 2nd ed., 34-66 (E.T. *From Tradition to Gospel*, 1934, 37-69). Strictly speaking, the description is valid only for the call-narratives in Mk, see 40f. (E.T. 43-46) and cf.108f. (E.T. 111f.). For Mt 8.19-22// he prefers the Greek form of the *Chreia*, 150ff. (E.T. 152ff.), cf.159 (E.T. 150ff.), which however is closely related to the paradigm. Cf. also the criticism of Bultmann's 'ideal scene' 160 (E.T. 156ff.).

at burials of the dead, as expressed say in Lucian's *Demonax* or *De luctu*;[11] within the framework of Jesus' proclamation, it hardly fits with this trend of thought, and it is extremely improbable that the community behind the Q tradition should have transformed a Cynic proverb of wounding and biting sharpness into a saying of Jesus.[12] By contrast with Cynic polemics the saying has no 'educative' tendency. We must similarly reject too the attempt of various exegetes to illuminate the backgrounds of this 'ideal scene' psychologically and in this to reflect on the state of the father *in extremis* – whether already dead, or mortally sick, or simply senile – or on Jesus' pedagogical intentions – say with an eye to the dangers of arguments over the inheritance; this only attenuates the sharpness of Jesus' answer, which is in fact emphasized by the extreme baldness of the scene, and wholly falsifies its central purpose.[13] It is of course true that there are already in the evangelists some traces of a psychological explanation: Matthew indirectly accounts for Jesus' rejection of the man by referring to the forthcoming journey across the lake, and Luke – not entirely incorrectly in the light of the facts of the matter – explains it by the missionary commission and the sending out of the disciples which immediately follows this.

[11] Cf. e.g. *Demonax* 65, the authentic Cynic answer of the dying philosopher to the question of his interment: 'The smell will bury me'; and, to the objection, whether he did not find it shameful to be eaten by dogs and birds: 'There is nothing unjust in my being of service to some living creatures once I am dead'. See H. D. Betz 'Lukian v. Samosata und das N.T.', TU 76 (1961), 74, 120f.; for further Cynic parallels see A. T. Ehrhardt, StTH 6 (1952) 131ff. Also E. Wechssler, *Hellas im Evangelium*, 1936, 259 places this saying, and the other *logia* on 'following after', against a Cynic background, see also below p.28f. and n.43.

[12] A. T. Ehrhardt, op.cit.130 draws attention to the *Scholion* on Euripides' *Andromache* 849 (not, as stated, *Alcestis* 894), ed. E. Schwartz 2, 304 line 3f.: οἱ γὰρ νεκροὶ μέλλουσι (vl. μέλουσι) τοῖς νεκροῖς ὡς οἱ ζῶντες τοῖς ζῶσι. There, of course, the subject is not interment, but relates only to the passage in *Andromache* which states that the dead person belongs to the dead (of the underworld). Even the relatively widespread summons in epitaphs to abandon fruitless lamenting for the dead, since the dead were better off than the living (cf. Lucian, *de luctu* 19f.; *Anth Gr* 7.48; 10.59; W. Peek, *Griechische Grabgedichte*, 1960, 158.7ff.; 304.5; 365.3f.), or the prohibition of gifts for the dead, 454.9ff., are to different effect. One might rather quote 182.6: ζώντων δ'οὐδὲν ἔχουσι νεκροί. As far as I can see the only person apart from Loisy, *L'Evangile selon Luc*, 1924, 288f., 'dicton proverbial' – ('proverbial maxim'), to assert that the logion does not go back to the historical Jesus is H. Braun, *Spätjudisch-häretischer und frühchristlicher Radikalismus*, BHTh 24, 2 (1957), 57 n.1 and he provides no additional justification for this. Cf. on the other hand R. Bultmann, op.cit. (n.9), 28 (E.T. 29) who says of Mt 8.22b 'it seems a matter of course that it refers to some specific occasion' – cf. also 110 (E.T. 105): like Lk 9.62 it belongs to the authentic sayings of Jesus which are 'the product of an energetic summons to repentance', see also *Die Erforschung d synopt. Evang.*, 1966 5th ed., 42. On the setting of the logion see also M. Dibelius, *Botschaft und Geschichte*, 1953, 1, 101.

[13] This holds good for most of the older commentaries. Typical of many of them would be, say, H. H. Wendt, *Die Lehre Jesu*, 1901, 2nd ed., 289f., or B. Weiss, *Mt*, MeyerK 1910, 9th ed., 174. Even F. Hauck, *Lk*, ThHK, 1934, 137 offers as justification the temptation of arguments over the inheritance. See also the discussion about whether what we have here is merely oriental periphrasis for the father's great age, in H. G. Howard, W. J. Davies and C. S.S. Ellison in ET 61 (1949/50), 350f. and 62 (1950/51), 92f.

Intrinsically, the disciple is asking for something completely obvious
and indeed necessary. His wish ἐπίτρεψόν μοι πρῶτον therefore does not
mean, as A. Schulz thought, that he has a false 'scale of values', the word
πρῶτον placing piety towards his father above Jesus' call[14] – to take this
line would only be to import an alien modern concept into the text. Jesus'
rejoinder shows rather the incommensurability of following him with all
human 'scales of value' and conceptions.

In terms of its outward form, Jesus' answer amounts to a paradoxically
formulated single-membered aphorism; by the word-play contained in it,
Jesus shows himself to be someone who formulates *ad hoc* maxims, and
this is something we find also in a great number of his other logia, and
something which is also true of the previous and subsequent maxims on
following him (Lk 9.58 and 9.62).[15] Here Jesus stands closer to the older
Jewish Wisdom say of Qoheleth and of Ben Sira, which still draws its life
from the 'directness of its vision of the world', than to his rabbinical
contemporaries. The impression we gain is that Jesus is deliberately
trying to provoke people by this sharp rejoinder of his; there is indeed a
similar tendency to be found in some pronouncements in Qoheleth,
whose words were compared by his disciple to 'ox-goads' and to 'nails
firmly fixed'.[16] Naturally it must not be overlooked here that, from the
standpoint of Jesus' eschatologically conditioned message, with its pressing for radical decision, his position is basically different in principle both
from the older Wisdom and from the rabbis. A saying like Mt 8.22,
despite its polished aphoristic form, can hardly be conceived of in the
mouth of a real 'teacher of wisdom'. Moreover all the attempts to trans-
late the saying back into Aramaic remain completely hypothetical and the
various self-contradictory proposals for taking the sting out of the offensive saying of Jesus by evidencing supposed errors in translation merely
show how wholly questionable such attempts are.[17]

The old dispute whether the first νεκρούς means literally 'people who

[14] A. Schulz, op.cit. (n.1), 107. The πρῶτον should probably be understood temporally,
see E. Klostermann *Mt* 77.
[15] See R. Bultmann, op.cit. (n.9), 80, 84 (E.T. 77, 81); G. Dalman, *Jesus-Jeschua*, 1922,
210 (E.T. 1929, 204ff.). On the subject see C. F. Burney *The Poetry of our Lord*, 1925,
passim, and 132, 169 on Mt 8.20// and 132, 170 on Lk 9.62, also M. Black, *An Aramaic
Approach to the Gospels*, 1954, 2nd ed., 105-142.
[16] Cf. already Ernst Käsemann's comment, EVuB 1, 209 (E.T. *Essays on N.T. Themes*,
1964, 4.1f.); see also below, p.46. On Qoheleth's provocative pronouncements see the 1st
epilogue, 12, 9-11, especially 11a.
[17] See F. Perles, ZNW 19 (1919/20), 96, followed by I. Abrahams, *Studies in Pharisaism
and the Gospels*, 1924, 2, 183. There is justified criticism of Perles in Bill 1.489. No better is
M. Black's proposal op.cit (n.20) 220 = ET 61 (1949/50), 219, or G. M. Lamsa's in *Die
Evangelien in Aramäischer Sicht*, 1963, 110f. On the problems of 'translation errors' see E.
Haenchen, *Der Weg Jesu*, 1966, 157; H. Ott, NovTest 9 (1967), 19ff., who draws attention
to the fact that it is not altogether certain that Jesus always spoke Aramaic. He could also
have used Mishnaic Hebrew, which was still a living language. Cf. previously J. Jeremias,
Abendmahlsworte Jesu, 1967, 4th ed., 189ff. (E.T. *The Eucharistic Words of Jesus*, 1966,
187ff., 196ff.).

are actually dead' or figuratively 'those who are spiritually dead', must probably be decided in favour of the latter sense, with Schlatter and Bultmann. The Synoptic tradition itself (Lk 15.24,32, cf. Mt 23.27), like the rest of the New Testament and Judaism and the Hellenistic world, was acquainted with a variety of figurative uses.[18] 'Dead buriers of the dead' are those who do not allow themselves to be affected by Jesus' message or by the nearness of the Kingdom. It is in hearing his word that the decision over life and death in the true sense is made. Both the early Church Fathers and Valentinian Gnosticism take up the double usage of the word νεκρούς. An allegorical interpretation also suggested itself to them, once again because it was thus possible to get round the offensiveness of the saying. In Marcion the logion was in addition used to devalue the body created by the demiurge.[19]

3 The break with law and custom

The saying, however, derives its unique sharpness from the fact that it could be understood not only as an attack on the respect for parents which is demanded in the fourth commandment[20] but also because at the same time it disregarded something which was at the heart of Jewish piety: *works of love*, which according to Ab 1.2 had an independent place alongside Torah and cultus and yet at the same time had their basis in the Torah. Under Ḥasidic-Pharisaic influence the last offices for the dead had gained primacy among all good works. For the dead in one's own family the saying in Ber 3.1a held good:

[18] A. Schlatter, *Der Evangelist Mt*, 289: 'the phrase would otherwise take on a scornful tone which runs counter to the profound seriousness of the question'. E. Schweizer, op.cit. (n.2) 14 n.38 is probably wrong in seeing it as an attempt 'to attenuate the intended paradox'. On the figurative meaning see Eph 2.1, 5; Col 2.13; 1 Tim 5.6; 1 Jn 3.14; Jewish parallels: see Sir 22.11f.; Bill 1.489 and 3.652; for the proselyte see also D. Daube, *The N.T. and Rabbinic Judaism*, 1956, 110, and *Jos. and Asen*, 20.7 (Batiffol 70). Further references in R. Bultmann, ThW 4, 896, 898 (E.T. 4.892-895) on the passage, also H. Hommel, ZNW 57 (1966), 10 n.36, who draws attention to Aristotle's saying in Diogenes Laertius 5, 19. We must reject the suggestion by T. M. Donn in ET 61 (1949/50), 384, that the saying was addressed to a third party and that the questioning disciple was himself intended as 'the dead', similarly to the Pythagoreans' considering as 'dead' a disciple who parted company with them, see below p.25 n.31.

[19] See Irenaeus 5.9.1: 'quoniam non habent Spiritum qui vivificat hominem': cf. 1.1.16 (1.8.3) among the Valentinians. Clem Alex *Strom* 4.135.5 links this with Homer, *Odyssey* 10.495. For Tertullian's explanation, *Adv Marc* 4.23.10, see below, p.11. There is a gnostic development in *Gospel of Philip* trsl. (Ger.) by H. M. Schenke in Leipoldt-Schenke, *Koptisch-Gnostiche Schriften*.... ThF 20 (1960), 38, saying 3. 'Those who inherit (κληρονομείν) the dead are themselves dead and inherit (κληρονομείν) the dead'. On Marcion, see Clem Alex *Strom* 3.25.3 and the passage from Tertullian quoted above; see also A. v. Harnack, *Marcion*, reprint of 2nd impression 1924 (1960), 205* and 300*.

[20] On the central meaning of the Fourth Commandment see Bill 1.705ff., 902f. (c) and 3.614. According to a relatively late tradition it was described as the weightiest or most difficult commandment.

He who is confronted by a dead relative is freed from reciting the Shema', from the Eighteen Benedictions, and from all the commandments stated in the Torah.

The duty to participate in a funeral procession could even override study of the Torah (see Billerbeck 4.560a) and the interment of a dead person without relatives, enjoined by the commandment (מֵת מִצְוָה), cancelled even the prohibition on pollution of the high priests and Nazarites by a corpse;[21] this is also an example of how even rabbinical tradition could limit the application of individual commands and prohibitions for reasons of humanity. The Mishnah Ed 8.4 and its explanation in AZ 37b show that this tendency to permit on humanitarian grounds specified relaxations of the regulations relating to corpse impurity is first attested for Jose b. Joezer during the early Maccabean period.[22] The Book of Tobit which came into being even somewhat earlier, should also be mentioned here. In it, the idea of the מֵת מִצְוָה is linked with the legendary motif of the grateful dead person. In addition, it shows, as do the entire literature of the Testaments of the Patriarchs and Josephus, that the request for interment by one's own son was a generally widespread, conventional motif behind which there lay a firmly established freely accepted custom.[23] Even Apollonius of Tyana, who is portrayed as being com-

[21] On the works of love see Bill 4.559-564; on the loving service of burying the dead and following the funeral procession, Bill 1.487ff. (see there also re those dead to whom one is in duty bound) and 4.578-592, here also a survey of burial customs. Alongside the funeral procession and the burial 'comforting the mourners' was a further special work of love, 4.592-607; previously came the visiting of the sick 573-578. All the basic attitudes are already well established in the Tannaitic period. On the exegetical justification for considering burial of the dead as a 'work of love', see MekEx 18.20 (Lauterbach 2.182), and Bill 4.560f. In Soṭa 14a (cf. SDtn 11.22 §49) works of love are explained as 'following God' (see below p.19 n.9) and in particular the burial of the dead is justified on the basis of Deut 34.6. Abraham, Moses and Daniel practised this work of love, see Bill 1.487a; 4.451f. c-e. On the extensive mourning and burial customs in Jewish Palestine see S. Klein, *Tod und Begräbnis in Palästina z. Zt. d. Tannaiten*, Diss. Freiburg, 1908, 18ff., 41ff.; and the testimony of Josephus, A. Schlatter, *Die Theologie des Judentums*... BFCTh 2. R.26 (1932), 162. The attitude in connection with this concrete point does not of course mean that Jesus had fundamentally rejected the substance behind the 'works of love'; on the contrary; see J. Jeremias, *Gleichnisse Jesu*, 1965, 7th ed., 204ff. (E.T. *The Parables of Jesus*, 2nd ed., 1963, 205ff.) and *Abba* 110-114 = ZNW 35 (1936), 77-81 (cf. E.T. *The Prayers of Jesus*, 1967, 66-82). However any casuistic legal codification was repugnant to him. The decisive thing is a faith that is put into practice ('living faith' – Jeremias, *Gleichnisse*, 207 E.T. 209). In the early Church the community's care for the burial of the poor had an essential part to play, see Aristides, *Apol* 15.8 (Goodspeed 21); Tertullian, *Apol* 39.6; generally the Jewish 'works of love' are continued in the caring activities of the ancient Church. On the subject see A. v. Harnack, *Mission u. Ausbreitung*... 1924, 4th ed., 1.177ff. and on burial in particular see 190ff.

[22] On the circumvention by the Rabbis of individual commandments which were no longer 'appropriate to the age' see Bill 1.717f.

[23] On the wish of parents to be buried by their sons, see Gen 49.29ff.; 50.1ff.; 50.25, and MekEx 13.19 (Lauterbach 1.176f.) and above all Tob 4.3f.; 6.15: καὶ υἱὸς ἕτερος οὐχ ὑπάρχει αὐτοῖς ὃς θάψει αὐτούς 14.9.11f. There is something very similar in *Bell* 5.545

pletely free of human prejudices and as condemning possessions and outward honours (see below pp.26f.) 'hurried, when he heard of his father's death, to Tyana, and interred him with his own hands beside his mother's grave' (Philostratus, *Vita Apoll* 1.13). Conversely, refusal of burial had always been considered among the Greeks and Jews as an unheard of act of impiety and as the severest of punishments for criminals; behind this lies the old and widespread animistic idea that the unburied dead could find no rest.[24] Basically there was on this point no difference between Jews and Gentiles: 'Burial of the dead was for the ancients always both a human and a religious duty' (E. Stommel, RAC 2.200).

Isolated parallels which could be quoted in relation to Jesus' strange and disconcerting attitude are only partially valid. Lev 21.11f. forbade the High Priest to be polluted by the corpses of his parents – perhaps in intensification of older stipulations like Lev 21.1f. and Ez 44.25ff. – and according to Num 6.6 this also held good for the Nazirites.[25] In the New

---

where Josephus' mother laments the (false) news of his death: ὑφ' οὗ ταφήσεσθαι προσεδόκησεν. The motif is widespread: see also Jub 23.7; 36.1f., 18 and the stereotyped conclusion in the Test 12: TReuben 7.1f.; TLevi 19.5 etc. Contrariwise non-burial of one's father or omission of the ceremonial for the dead is desecration, see syr Aḥikar 15, Charles AP 2.749, cf. Pes 4.9a. Giessener Mishna (ed. G. Beer): Hezekiah desecrates the bones of his father Ahaz; see also the mitigation of this offensive behaviour offered in the interpretation of it in Sanh 47a: to make atonement for his father.

[24] See *Epic of Gilgamesh* 12.155ff.; ANET 99; *Odyssey* 11.51ff., 72ff., cf. L. Dürr-L. Koep, RAC 2.194ff. and E. Stommel 2.200f. Prohibition of family mourning for criminals guilty of a capital crime was considered to be particularly cruel: Suetonius, *Tib* 61.2 and refusal of burial was considered to be even worse: see E. Rhode, *Psyche*, 2nd ed., 1.217f. and Suetonius, *Vesp* 2.3 under Caligula. Non-burial as a punishment for the godless man occurs in prophetic threats, particularly in Jeremiah, see G. Fohrer, ZAW 78 (1966), 39: cf. 1 En 98.13; 2 Macc 5.10; Jos, *Ant* 10.97; *Bell* 2.465; 3.377; 4.317, 385. The positive counterpart is given by Sir 44.4; 46.12; 49.10 and the related veneration of the graves of holy men in Jewish Palestine in the Hellenistic period, see J. Jeremias, *Heiligengräber in Jesu Umwelt*, 1958 and ZNW 52 (1961), 96-101. Even the tale of the grateful dead man in Tobit (see O. Eissfeldt, *Einleitung in das A.T.*, 1964, 3rd ed., 791f. (E.T., *The Old Testament: an Introduction*, 1965, 584) and the specifically Jewish idea of מֵת מִצְוָה should be understood against this background. For a detailed discussion see M. A. Beek in *Pro Regno Pro Sanctuario, Festschrift for G. v. d. Leeuw*, 1950, 19-29, who also draws attention to the offensiveness of Mt 8.22 in this connection. The tale of the grateful dead man appears in two versions in H. Schmidt-P. Kahle, *Volkserzählungen aus Palästina*, 1918, 85-99, and in each case a living person who protects a corpse from desecration is rewarded by the resurrected dead person. There is no relevance to our logion in the Egyptian tale (cited by H. Gressmann on Mt 8.22 in *Protestantenblatt* 49 (1916), 281) about a dead man who sees to his own burial. However it is peculiar that Mt 8.22 is on a secondary level linked in the *Acts of Peter* with the motif of the 'grateful dead': see *Mart Petr* 11 ed. Lipsius 1.100 (101), where Peter appears after his execution to Marcellus, who had attended to his burial, and reminds him of Jesus' saying: ἄφετε τοὺς νεκροὺς θάπτεσθαι ὑπὸ τῶν ἰδίων νεκρῶν . . . σὺ γὰρ ζῶν ὑπάρχων ὡς νεκρὸς νεκροῦ ἐπεμελήθης. Perhaps there is a proverb behind this, see above, n.17.

[25] See on this K. Elliger, *Leviticus* HAT 1966, 278, 282, 298. According to this Lev 21.1b-4 belongs to the material available to the Ph² redactor, who inserted 21.10-15 for extra emphasis.

Testament period however there existed all along the line the contrasting tendency to curtail the scope of these stipulations. Siphra Lev on 21.11 excludes from this commandment the dead to whom one has an obligation but also on Num 21.3 reports from the period of the Second Temple that the scribes forcibly made unclean a priest whose wife had died on passover eve, though he had not wished to make himself unclean, so that he could eat the passover sacrifice. Equally the exegesis of Lev 21.11 in Philo clearly shows an anti-ritual bias.[26] The commandment relating to the high priest and the Nazarites can therefore hardly, as Schniewind argues, be adduced as motivating Jesus' answer, as a cultic and ritual basis for his demand was – in contrast, say, to the Essenes – in any case far from his thoughts.[27] To be sure this connection is not a new one, for we find it already in a very instructive context in Tertullian (adv Marc 4.23, 10f.), where in his struggle against Marcion's rejection of the Old Testament he sees a confirmation of the Mosaic Law in Jesus' demand in Lk 9.60.

Tertullian thinks that Jesus' saying, 'utramque legem creatoris manifeste confirmavit: et de sacerdotio in Levitico, prohibentem sacerdotes supremis etiam parentum interesse . . . et de devotione in Arithmis; nam et illi, qui se deo voverit, inter cetera iubet, ne super ullam animam introeat defunctam, ne super patris quidem aut matris aut fratris.' The additional justification exhibits a tendency, fraught with consequences, to base the 'commission' to preach on the Old Testament institutions: 'Puto autem, et devotioni et sacerdotio destinabat, quem praedicando regno dei imbuerat.' Without this background (nulla ratione legis intercedente) Jesus' demand would be 'satis impius'. Similarly Tertullian the lawyer also bases on the 'Law' the saying about the man who turns back after putting his hand to the plough, by dint of the cautionary example of Lot's wife in Gen 19.17.

Jesus' answer, which in a unique way expresses his sovereign freedom in respect of the Law of Moses and of custom in general among Jews and Greeks, is here turned upside down so as to carry a contrasting sense; it has to confirm the Law and derives its authentication from the Law.

On the other hand two examples from the *prophets* lead us further. In Ezekiel 24.15-24 Yahweh forbids the prophet to lament the dead and to carry out the mourning ritual on the occasion of his wife's decease. This

[26] See Bill 1.488f., cf. Zeb 100a. Philo, *Spec Leg* 1.113-116, no longer has a ritual justification for this prohibition, but points rather to the total turning of the High Priest to the sanctuary and to his supraterrestrial position as a mediator between man and God. According to *Fuga* 109.113, it is applied allegorically to the Logos, the Son of God and to Wisdom, who is set apart from every 'dead soul' i.e. all evil. Manifest is the tendency to relax this ritual stipulation or to give it a spiritualizing interpretation.

[27] *Das Evg. n. Mt.* NTD 1950, 4th ed., 114. On Jesus' rejection of ritualism see H. Braun, op.cit. (n.12), 2.65f. and *Qumran und das N.T.* 1966, 1.29. Jesus is bordering on tendencies of Greek-speaking Judaism in his anti-ritualist equation of 'uncleanness' with an 'evil heart', see F. Hauck, ThW 3.420f. (E.T. 3.413ff.); 4.648 n.14 (E.T. 4.644); 649 n.7 (E.T. 4.646), cf. also Heb 7.26 and 12.15.

extremely disconcerting behaviour on the part of the prophet is intended
to intimate judgment against God's people as a 'sign' (מוֹפֵת). Similarly
Yahweh demands of Jeremiah abstention from marriage (Jer 16.1-4, cf.
on the other hand Deut 7.14 and Is 4.1), participation in banquets and
jovial gatherings (16.8f.) and further forbids him to visit a house of
mourning and take part in lamentations for the dead (16.5-7). This
'anti-social' behaviour is also meant to serve the purpose of proclaiming
the coming judgment, for God is withdrawing from his people his 'good
pleasure' (חֶסֶד). Of course, these 'parabolic actions' of the prophets do
not constitute direct parallels, but they do show how Yahweh, to advert-
ise his own future activities, could demand from individual prophets a
rigorous break with the taboos and conventions of their environment,
even specifically here, as regards customs relating to mourning. If Jesus
demanded even more incisively of his prospective follower that he should
override the fourth commandment and the 'works of love', he was
demanding this, basically, in way in which in the Old Testament only God
himself enjoined obedience on individual prophets in regard to the pro-
calmation of his approaching judgment.[28]

Individual analogies from the Hellenistic field are hardly comparable
with Jesus' situation. Thus C. Schneider draws attention to the Catochus
Ptolemaeus in Memphis, who could not leave the Serapeum when his
father died 'for the sake of Serapis'. Here, however, we have basically a
sort of enforced confinement by which Ptolemaeus was kept there against
his will.[29] And the speech quoted by H. Hommel, made against Socrates
by his accusers in Xenophon, according to which Socrates described the
corpses of his ancestors and of other close kindred as something 'useless
and serving no purpose' and rightly to be buried as soon as possible,[30]
points in another direction. The same is true of the request by the
philosopher and martyr that there be no fuss made about his corpse or his
burial (*Phaedo* 115c-e, cf. Ign, *Rom* 4.2 and Lucian, *Demonax* 66). Jesus,
of course, is not arguing rationally about the uselessness of a corpse but is
in sovereign fashion breaking down the barrier of respect for the dead and
of custom. A real analogy which we shall have to investigate, does indeed
exist in the fact that in this context the accusation is made against Socrates
that he was educating his pupils to condemn their ancestors and relations

[28] I owe to Prof. Gese the references to Ezekiel and Jeremiah. Cf. perhaps also Ezek
4.9-15; 12.1-7; Hos 1.2ff.; Is 20.1-6 where Jahweh as a sign of his coming activity in judging
demands from his prophets in each case an action of a very curious kind.

[29] Cf. C. Schneider, *Geistesgeschichte des Christentums*, 1954, 1.38. See in this connection U. Wilckens, UPZ 1.125 No. 4, 8 and cf. p.55. The text is extremely fragmentary;
Wilcken's restoration of it is questionable: [τοῦ δὲ πατρό]ς μ [ου] εἰς θεοὺς μετελθόντος/
[ἐμοῦ δὲ χάρ]ιν [το]ῦ Σαράπιος χωρισθῆναι [οὐ δυναμένο]υ. A divergent reconstruction
with a similar sense is given by L. Delekat, *Katochē, Hierodulie und Adoptionsfreilassung*,
MBPAR 47 (1964), 52ff.

[30] See H. Hommel, ZNW 57 (1966), 12f., cf. *Memor* 1.2.53-55; and op.cit. 13 n.48, the
Heraclitan fragment 96 (Diels-Kranz, *Fragm. d. Vorsokratiker*, 1964, 11th ed., 1.172) and
14f., the Aristotle quotation on the uselessness of the corpse.

(πατέρας... καὶ... συγγενεῖς ἐποίει ἐν ἀτιμίᾳ εἶναι παρὰ τοῖς ἑαυτῷ συνοῦσι), *Memorabilia*, 1.2.51; see below p.29f., n.46-48.

The key to this consciously provocative reply by Jesus is to be sought in specific sayings of his which are likewise probably connected with his call to follow him – as when in Mt 10.37 (// Lk 14.26) he demands complete freedom from all family ties for the disciple,[31] as he himself also at least for the time being had broken with his family (Mk 3.21: ὅτι ἐξέστη – see below, p.64) and, against general Jewish custom, had remained unmarried, like an Elijah or a Jeremiah.[32] The background to such sayings is to be found in the prophetic, apocalyptic motif of the destruction of the family in the period of the final eschatological 'peirasmos' (Mic 7.6; Zech 13.3; 1 En 99.5; 100.1f.; Jub 23.16; syr Bar 70.6 and Mk 13.12// and Lk 12.53 = Mt 10.35 Q). Even if the formulation of these logia is due to the community tradition, the basic idea probably goes back to Jesus himself (Mt 10.34 = Lk 12.51): decision for Jesus does not bring peace but disruption (διαμερισμός) to families.[33]

We might here draw attention to the fact that the Essenes too – appealing perhaps to passages like Deut 33.9 – demanded that the intending novice should break with his family[34] but the novice thereby entered the esoteric, self-contained, ritually pure circle of the true Israel and holy remnant – which was complete in its obedience to the Law, while Jesus did not in fact make such a separation from the people as a whole.[35] The reason *why* Jesus demanded this break with the family, with respect for one's forebears and with custom remains therefore initially unexplained. This is already enough to demonstrate the improbability of A. Schulz's view that the call to follow is to be understood as the

---

[31] Cf. also Mk 1.20b: καὶ ἀφέντες τὸν πατέρα αὐτῶν Ζεβεδαῖον ἐν τῷ πλοίῳ μετὰ τῶν μισθωτῶν ἀπῆλθον ὀπίσω αὐτοῦ. On the ἀφιέναι and ἀκολουθεῖν motif in Mk see below p.33 n.60. We must not, as K. H. Rengstorf, *Das Evg. n. Lc*, NTD 1966, 11th ed., 131 and G. Schrenk, ThW 5.982 (E.T. 5.982) try to do, deprive of its force the annulment of the Fourth Commandment through Jesus' call to follow him, by appealing to sayings like Mk 7.10ff.// or Mk 10.19//. Jesus' call really does cancel out for the concrete moment the 'natural ties' and 'the duty to honour one's parents', cf. M. Dibelius – W. G. Kümmel, *Jesus*, 1966, 4th ed., 48: 'because the decision for the Kingdom does not admit of that "but first" element'.

[32] See Mk 3.20f., 31-35//: cf. Lk 11.27f.; Jn 2.3f.; 7.3ff. On Jesus' unmarried state see Mt 19.12 and H. Windisch op.cit. (p.25 n.31) 130ff.

[33] See G. Schrenk, ThW 5.983 (E.T. 5.982f.). The apocalyptic motif was aroused through the split in the people connected with the Hellenistic attempt at reform under Antiochus IV Epiphanes and the Maccabaean revolt: see also below p.19 n.13.

[34] See 4 QTest 16ff. (E. Lohse, *Die Texte von Qumran*, 1964, 250) cf. also O. Betz, op.cit. (n.2), 47f., who refers to 1 QS 6.2f., 19f.; 1 QH 4.8f. and Josephus, *Bell* 2.120ff.; see especially 122: μίαν ὥσπερ ἀδελφοῖς ἅπασιν οὐσίαν and 134: having recourse to relatives is allowed only with the agreement of the overseer. This particular form of Essene rigorism with its hostility to the family was not found however in all the groups, see CD, *Bell* 2.160ff. and as regards the age of salvation 1 QSa. C. G. Montefiore, *The Synoptic Gospels*, 1927, 2.133 refers to Deut 33.9 in connection with Mt 8.22 and adds 'The verse was, however, practically ignored by the Jewish tradition and feeling'.

[35] See H. Braun, *Qumran u. das N.T.*, 1966, 2.93ff.

establishment of a teacher-pupil relationship between Jesus and his disciples on the analogy of the activities of a rabbinical school. For a Jewish
family it was, rather, an honour, when one of its members was deemed
worthy of becoming 'the pupil of a scribe', for the scribe, by his knowledge and his legal decisions generally attained to a higher social
position.[36] The few anecdotes which – in a certain analogy to the Greek
philosophical call-narrative – tell of a protest by the family against entry
into the 'school', end with a reconciliation justified by the honour which
will accrue to the scholar (see below p.32 n.56). Following Jesus, on the
other hand, brought neither honour nor a higher social status. If in
Matthew's account, 8.19, the first question about following Jesus is put by
a 'scribe', this is perhaps because he wishes to reject the mistaken application of a rabbinical view of discipleship to following Jesus. Such a view,
which was in accord with its day and age, is here rejected by Jesus'
discouraging answer, for following Jesus was diametrically opposed to
the peaceful, secure atmosphere of the rabbinical school (see below,
pp.53f., n.58).

There is hardly one logion of Jesus which more sharply runs counter to
law, piety and custom than does Mt 8.22 = Lk 9.60a, the more so as here
we cannot justify the overriding of these in the interests of humanitarian
freedom, higher morality, greater religious intensity or even 'neighbour-
liness'. The saying is completely incompatible with the old liberal picture
of Jesus and with more modern attempts to resuscitate this. The unique
offensiveness of Mt 8.22 was clearly expressed, particularly by A.
Schlatter. 'That *pietas* could be denied at this point, and the duty of a son
overridden, was completely unthinkable to Jewish sensitivities. It was a
purely sacrilegious act of impiety. . . . Such sayings could easily suggest to
the disciples the thought that Jesus was abolishing the Law.'[37]

---

[36] See e.g. j. Hag 77b, 32ff. (Bill 2.603). The wealthy father of the later apostate Elisha b.
Abuyah said on the day of his circumcision 'if the power of the Torah is so great, I will
destine this my son for the Torah if he remains alive. . .' See also Ned 50a and Keth 62b (cf.
ARN Vs A c. 6.ed., Schechter, p.28f.): the herd Akiba b. Joseph marries the daughter of his
master on condition that he studies the Torah. Because of this *mésalliance* he casts out the
pair and disinherits the daughter. However, when Akiba returns a famous scholar, he is
reconciled to him. Study of the Torah was for a simple Jew one way of becoming respected
and often well-to-do, and the fate of Hillel was a typical example of this. Cf. also Ab 6.1, 2,
7; BB 10.8b; see below p.34f. To be sure opportunism as a reason for studying the Law and
scholarship as a means of acquiring gain were despised, but in practice they could never be
wholly excluded. On the scribes as part of the upper classes, see J. Jeremias, *Jerusalem zur
Zeit Jesu*, 1962, 3rd ed., II B 101ff. (265ff.) (E.T. *Jerusalem in the Time of Jesus*, 1969,
112ff., 233ff.). The power of their knowledge and their prestige among the people generally
resulted in an improvement in their social status. The fact is that Hillel did not remain a
day-labourer all his life, and his descendants, the Patriarchs of later days, also became the
richest Jews in Palestine. The polemics in Mt 23.1-36 also show the Pharisees and Scribes to
be a group on a higher social level than the ordinary people.

[37] A. Schlatter, *Der Evangelist Mt*, 288, cf. also E. Hirsch, *Frühgeschichte des Evangeliums*, 1941, 2.97 – 'something which was wholly and simply new' – and G. Schrenk, ThW
5.982 (E.T. 5.982).

One is thus led to suppose that this relentless hardness on Jesus' part as to the unconditional nature of following him can no longer primarily be understood from the standpoint of the effectiveness of Jesus as a 'teacher', but it is to be explained only on the basis of his unique authority as the proclaimer of the *imminent Kingdom of God*. In the light of its urgent proximity, there was no more time to be lost and so he had to be followed without procrastination and to the abandonment of all human considerations and ties.[38] The phenomenon must therefore be investigated no longer only in relation to the teacher-pupil relationship on the lines of the rabbinical parallels but above all from an *eschatological* angle and – must we not say? – in the light of the *messianic authority of Jesus*.

[38] On Jesus' temporal expectation of the coming of the Kingdom in the near future, see E. Grässer, *Das Problem der Parusieverzögerung*..., BZNW 22 (1960, 2nd ed.), 3-75 and especially 74. Cf. also W. G. Kümmel, *Verheissung u. Erfüllung*, AThANT 6 (1956, 3rd ed.) passim (E.T. *Promise and Fulfilment*, 1957, passim) and 'Die Naherwartung in der Verkündigung Jesu', in *Heilsgeschehen in Geschichte (HuG)*, Ges. Aufs., 1965, 457-470. Attempts to deny this state of affairs, as recently by Bammel, op.cit. (n.9), 1-32, are in no way convincing because of the violence they do to the subject-matter.

II. Considerations from *Religionsgeschichte* relating to the charismatic and eschatological background of following Jesus

1 The prototype of Elisha's call by Elijah

We have already drawn attention to the strong influence exercised on the pericopae on following Jesus which we find in Mark and Q by Elisha's call at the hands of Elijah in 1 Kings 19.19-21. Elijah calls Elisha away from the twelve yokes of oxen with which he is ploughing and forbids him – according to the original point of the story[1] – to say farewell to his parents. Elisha slaughters his yoke of oxen as a sacrificial meal: וַיָּקָם וַיֵּלֶךְ אַחֲרֵי אֵלִיָּהוּ וַיְשָׁרְתֵהוּ 'and stood up and followed Elijah and served him'. It is above all, in Josephus' reproduction of the story in *Ant* 8.354, that the 'charismatic' understanding of this episode and the links with the Synoptic tradition of 'following' become discernible: When Elijah threw his magic cloak (see below, n. 71) over him, Elijah at once began to prophesy *(εὐθέως προφητεύειν ἤρξατο)*, left the oxen and followed Elijah *(καταλιπὼν τοὺς βόας ἠκολούθησεν Ἠλίᾳ)*. The Old Testament statement is indeed weakened by the fact that Elijah permits him to say farewell to his parents (the term *ἀποτάττεσθαι* appears, as in Lk 9.61), but then 'he followed *(εἵπετο)* and was Elijah's pupil *(μαθητής)* and servant *(διάκονος)* during the latter's entire life.'[2] The abandonment of family and possessions, the gift of prophecy, pupilhood and service are here closely inter-connected. In this connection it is striking that Elisha according to Josephus receives his prophetic gift as early as the time of his call while according to 2 Kings 2.9f., 15 – which Josephus handles only very baldly at *Ant.* 9.27f. – it is passed on to him only just before Elijah is snatched away. An analogous contrast may be said to exist between the transmission of authority in Lk 9.1 and the promise in 24.48f.

Josephus' positive interpretation in relation to the question of Elisha's leaving his parents gives grounds for supposing that in Jesus' day the passage was so interpreted and that consequently both Mt 8.21f. and Lk 9.61f. should be understood as imposing more radical demands than were imposed at the call of Elisha.[3] Despite all the things they have in common,

---

[1] See G. Fohrer, *Elia*, AThANT 31 (1957), 21f., cf. already A. Jepsen, *Nabi*, 1934, 78 n.2. As against Ex 4.18f an intensification is involved.

[2] Compare on the other hand the essentially simpler version in the LXX III Reg 19.20f.: κατέλιπεν... τὰς βόας καὶ κατέδραμεν ὀπίσω Ἠλίου... 21: καὶ ἐπορεύθη ὀπίσω Ἠλίου καὶ ἐλειτούργει αὐτῷ. On the subject itself see K. H. Rengstorf, ThW 4.442 ll. 15ff. (E.T. 4.429 ll. 18ff.), cf. also *Ant* 9.28, 33 and *Bell* 4.460.

[3] The LXX already corrects the statement in 𝔐; see A. Schulz, *Nachfolgen*, 101f., n.92.

16

however, attention must be drawn to *one* essential difference between the call to follow Jesus and the story of Elijah and Elisha, and this difference basically applies to all Old Testament call-narratives. There, the *person who calls* is ultimately *God* himself: whether he is commissioning a prophet to his vocation (1 Kings 19.15-18; Sam 16.1ff.; 1 Kings 11.31ff.) or whether he himself is calling through the medium of a vision (see below, p.73). Jesus' call to follow him cannot on the other hand be traced back to any other source; according to the Synoptics' account the call is empowered by Jesus' own *messianic authority*. On the other hand it is doubtless no accident that the 'classic' tale of Elisha's call by Elijah plays practically no part in Rabbinic tradition although Elijah and Elisha are frequently used among the rabbis to exemplify the teacher-pupil relationship.[4]

The – as far as I can see – sole mention of the call in the early Tannaitic period serves the purpose of illustrating the installation by lot of the Zealot high priest Phinehas from Haphta during the Jewish revolt after 66 A.D., Phinehas being compared with Elisha at the plough.[5] We must refrain from going more closely into the multifarious links between the Synoptic tradition about Jesus and the tales about Elijah and Elisha.[6] We may simply draw attention in the by-going to the fact that the powerfully effective saying of Jesus in Mk 1.17//Mt 4.19 δεῦτε ὀπίσω μου occurs in IV (II) Kings 6.19 (LXX = לְכוּ אַחֲרַי) in the mouth of Elisha, whereby he delivers a Syrian force into the power of the King of Israel. Significantly, we find no further instances in the Old Testament for the 'following' of his teacher by the pupil (of a prophet). On the occasion of Elijah's last journey with Elisha before he is snatched up in 2 Kings 2.1-12 we find rather: 'and the two went together' (וַיֵּלְכוּ שְׁנֵיהֶם). There may perhaps be a further reference to a teacher-pupil relationship in 2 Kings 4.38: '. . . and the disciples of the prophets sat before (Elisha)' (וּבְנֵי הַנְּבִיאִים יֹשְׁבִים לְפָנָיו). But here, perhaps, what is referred to is the typically

---

Thus the question left open by E. Schweizer *Erniedrigung*, 14 could be answered by saying that one should start as far as possible from the contemporary meaning of Old Testament texts where these are used in the N.T.

[4] Above all in the Seder Eliyahu rabbah ed. Friedmann passim, cf. e.g. c.5, p.23; c.17, p.86f. or Seder Eliyahu zuta c.2, p.173. Also e.g. Ber 7b Bar in the name of R. Simeon b. Johai (II Kings 3.11), MekEx 13.19 (Lauterbach 1.177); Elisha, the 'talmîd' of Elijah and Moses, the 'teacher (רב) of Elijah'; Sanh 68a, the exclamation of R. Akiba in the funeral procession for his teacher Eliezer b. Hyrcanus (II Kings 2.12); in which connection we should remember that the 'charismatic-zealot' element was still relatively strong in the case of Akiba and his teacher (who was excommunicated for his independent attitudes); see A. Guttmann HUCA 20 (1947), 374-388 and M. Hengel, *Die Zeloten*, AGSU 1 (1961), 113, 207, 245f., 295f.

[5] T. Yoma 1.6 (p.180). // Sifra Lev 21.10, and see M. Hengel, op.cit. 225 and below n.12, cf. also MekEx 12.1 (Lauterbach 1.9), justifying the call of Elisha 'in place of' Elijah by criticism of Elijah's (zealous) prophecy.

[6] See R. Meyer, *Der Prophet aus Galiläa*, 1940, 31-37, cf. also L. Goppelt, *Typos*, BFCTh 2nd series, 43 (1939), 86-89.

oriental phenomenon of the pupil's sitting in front of his teacher (compare Ab 1.4 and Acts 22.3). Outside the Elijah-Elisha cycle, the 'disciples of the prophets' appear relatively seldom (2 Kings 2.3 5, 15; 4.1; 5.22; 6.1; 9.1; cf. also Amos 7.14). Perhaps most impressive is Is 8.16:

> I will bind up the testimony,
> and seal the instruction by my disciples
> (on the basis of Kaiser's ATD translation).

Here the prophet Isaiah confronts us as the teacher of a group of pupils (limmudāi; note the first person singular suffix). In 8.18 on the other hand he points to his own physical children as 'a sign and portent' for Israel. Significantly – and this corresponds to the understanding in the Wisdom Literature of the teacher-pupil relationship as a 'spiritual father-son link', the rabbinic exegetical tradition and in all likelihood also the Targum on the passage sees the 'children' as the pupils of the prophets (jSanh 28b btm; Gen R 42.2; Lev R 11.7; Esth R Prol § 11.3 &c.: talmîdâw and Tg Is 8.11 'ulêmayya: young men; references in Bill 3.683). The discussion on the passage shows that it was related to the 'synagogues and schools' which Ahaz is said to have forbidden. It is a typical example of *interpretatio rabbinica* of the Old Testament prophetic tradition.[6a]

2 'Following' the charismatic-prophetic leader in Holy War

There is however still a further range of meaning for the concept of 'following' (הָלַךְ אַחֲרֵי or even just אַחֲרֵי = LXX ὀπίσω connected with another verb of movement) which we must look at: the *following of warriors behind their general in an army*, which could be understood in ancient Israel as, among other things, obedience to the call of a *charismatic leader* sent by God at a time of extreme emergency and of his messengers.[7] We find this motif with Ehud[8] and with Barak who follows the invitation of the prophetess Deborah, and here in archaic fashion Jahweh himself marches in front. Here we may have the original source of the idea of 'going behind' Jahweh which also sometimes appears in the Old Testament. This is a usage which gains significance above all in Deuteronomy and also requires to be considered.[9] Other charismatic

---

[6a] On 'spiritual parenthood' see L. Dürr in *Heilige Überlieferung, Festschrift I. Herwegen*, ed. O. Casel, 1938, 1-20.

[7] On military 'following' in general see Judg 9.4, 49: Abimelech; I Sam 17.13, 14: Saul; I Sam 30.21: David etc. On the 'charismatic' character of the military hero and judge in Israel see Max Weber, *Ges. Aufs. z. Religionssoziologie*, Bd 3, 1932, 2nd ed., 23, 47f., 52f., 93f.

[8] Judg 3.28: רִדְפוּ אַחֲרַי and רַיֵּרְדוּ אַחֲרָיו (καταβαίνετε ὀπίσω μου).

[9] Judg 4.14, cf. 2 Sam 5.24 and Ex 13.21ff. In the figurative sense see Deut 13.5; 1 Kings 14.8; 18.21; 2 Kings 23.3 = II Chron 34.31; cf. also Jer 2.2 (gloss?); Hos 11.10 and Josh 3.3f. The much more frequent negative expression 'running after other gods' has certainly suppressed to a great extent the positive usage. See G. Kittel, ThW1 211f. (E.T. 1.210ff.), cf. also H. Kosmala, ASTI 3 (1964), 64ff. On the difficulties caused by the idea of 'following

generals also appear, viz. Gideon[10] and above all Saul after the call for help from the men of Jabesh Gilead. Saul threatens all those who do not follow him and Samuel with severe punishment.[11] Here too the interpretation in Josephus *Ant* 6.77 is instructive: εἰ μὴ ... ἀκολουθήσουσιν αὐτῷ καὶ Σαμουήλῳ τῷ προφήτῃ ὅπου ποτ' ἂν αὐτοὺς ἀγάγωσι. This reminds us of the promise of the intending disciple in Mt 8.19 = Lk 9.57 (Q): ἀκολουθήσω σοι ὅπου ἐὰν ἀπέρχῃ. It is of significance that the 'charismatic leaders' are, rather like the prophets, called out of their normal calling by a special *vocatio*.[12]

This 'charismatic' call to follow the leader in a war of liberation waged for the sacred possessions of the people is linked with the demand to give up *safety* and *possessions* for the sake of God's cause. It appears again at the start of the Maccabaean revolt: thus, in 1 Macc 2.27ff., after slaying a Jew, who was willing to sacrifice to a pagan God, along with the Seleucid officer in charge, Mattathias calls to his fellow-citizens in these words: 'Let every one who is zealous for the Law and supports the covenant *follow after me.* And he fled with his sons into the mountain country and they *left all their possessions* behind in the town' (πᾶς ὁ ζηλῶν τῷ νόμῳ καὶ ἱστῶν διαθήκην ἐξελθέτω ὀπίσω μου· καὶ ἔφυγεν αὐτὸς καὶ οἱ υἱοὶ αὐτοῦ εἰς τὰ ὄρη καὶ ἐγκατέλιπον ὅσα εἶχον ἐν τῇ πόλει). Mattathias' action and the call he issues are described with all the features of a charismatic act; the struggle for freedom then beginning is a holy war. Alongside Phinehas the great prototype here is above all the zeal of Elijah.[13] The book of Daniel which came into existence shortly thereafter and the vision of animals in 1 Enoch which glorifies the struggle for freedom on the part of the Maccabees makes it reasonable to suppose

after God' among the later rabbis, see op.cit. 80ff. cf. I. Abrahams, op.cit. (p.7 n.17), 138-182. See also below p.27 n.39.

[10] Judg 6.34f.: 'But the spirit of the Lord clothed (לָבְשָׁה) Gideon; and he sounded the trumpet and Abiezer was called out to follow him' (אַחֲרָיו "א וַיִּזָּעֵק LXX ἐβόησεν A. ὀπίσω αὐτοῦ) cf. v. 35, where the same thing happens in the case of Manasseh through the medium of his messengers.

[11] I Sam 11.6f. The spirit of God comes on Saul, and he cuts a yoke of oxen in pieces (cf. I Kings 19.21) and sends them by messengers to Israel with the threat 'Whoever does not come out after Saul and Samuel, so shall it be done to his oxen' (אֲשֶׁר אֵינֶנּוּ יֹצֵא אַחֲרֵי שׁ׳ וְאַחֲרֵי שׁ׳).

[12] Cf. Judg 6.11f.: Gideon while 'beating out wheat': I Sam 11.5ff.: Saul returning from working in the fields, and a second, later tradition in I Sam 9.10: Saul looking for the asses; I Sam 16: David the shepherd. Cf. also I Kings 11.29ff.; 19.16f. = 2 Kings 9.1-13 and 9.18f., the ἐπιστρέφου εἰς τὰ ὀπίσω μου, also I Sam 3 and Amos 7.14f. Examples from outside Israel for the 'call' of primeval kings are in A. Jeremias, *Handbuch der altorientalischen Geisteskultur,* 1929, 2nd ed., 304; for the Greek world see also E. Wechssler, op.cit. (p.6 n.11), 260. Nowhere, of course do we have reports of 'calls' of such telling brevity as those in Mk 1.16ff. and 2.13f. Above all no actual call-narratives as such are known to the rabbis, see below p.50f. The nearest thing to it would be the anecdote about the High Priest Phinehas from Haphta. This is to an extent parallel to I Kings 19.19ff. and to the legend of the call of Cincinnatus from the plough to be dictator: see PW 24. 1021 and above p.17, n.5. On 'calls' in the realm of philosophy see below p.27.

[13] Cf. I Macc 1.26, 50, 58: see M. Hengel, op.cit. (n.4), 155ff., 175ff., 278f.

that a large number of those who revolted understood the rising also as a final time of testing prior to the dawn of the Kingdom of God. *The charismatic and the eschatological element are here conjoined.*[14]

From then on there repeatedly appeared in Palestine charismatic leader-figures who initiated popular movements – mostly with an eschatological orientation. It is true that the concept of 'following after' (הלךְאחרי) plays no positive part in the Essene community which came into being around 150 B.C. – we hear rather, in regard to the Teacher of Righteousness, only of 'hearkening to his words' which is the Hebrew equivalent for 'obeying', or of loyalty to him, while entry into the community is indirectly referred to as entry into the covenant (בוא בברית or עבר).[15] Nevertheless in CD 4.18ff. there is a sharp polemic against the 'builders of the wall' who 'follow after' a false prophet bearing the 'cover-name' of *Zaw*, taken from Is 28.10,13(בוני החוץ אשר הלכו אחרי צו) who falsifies the law as a deceiving 'preacher'. In CD 19.31f. we hear of God's abhorrence of the 'builders of the wall and of all who follow after them' (ובכל ההלכים אחריהם). There are good reasons for the supposition of A. S. van der Woude and R. Meyer that these opponents were the Pharisees, who in the first third of the first century B.C. gained sizeable influence among the people under their great leader Simeon ben Shetaḥ. The designations צו and מטיף הכזב or the like lead us to suppose that it was also possible for Simeon ben Shetaḥ to be considered as a charismatic figure, as the prophetic element in early Pharisaism seems to have been substantially greater than among the later rabbis, although even among the Tannaites of the first to the third generation it was still not wholly lacking.[16]

3 Apocalyptic prophets and Zealot leaders of the people in 1st century Palestine and their call to men to follow them

One gains the impression that first century Palestine was particularly fruitful soil for prophetic-charismatic movements of an eschatological

[14] See Dan 11.33ff.; and more positively I En 90.9-19.

[15] On the 'teacher': 1 QpHab 2.2(?); 8.3; CD 20.28,32; entrance into the covenant: 1QS 1 and 2 *passim*, cf. 5.7, 20; 6.15 and frequently. This 'entrance' was repeatedly renewed in the doxology cf. 1QS 10.10.

[16] On the prophetic origin of the term 'preacher of lies' (מטיף הכזב and similarly in CD 8.13, cf. 1.14; 4.19; 19.25f. and 1QpHab 10.9) see Mic 2.6,11; Amos 7.16; Ezek 21.2, 7. Might the designation 'Zaw' as in Is 28.10 refer to glossolalia among the 'builders of the wall'? Cf. perhaps also Hippolytus, *refut* 8.4 GCS ed. Wendland 89.20ff. On Simeon b. Shetaḥ see Schürer 1.279ff., 289ff. The entirely legendary texts about him are given by K. Schlesinger, *Die Gesetzeslehrer*, 1936, 39-61; cf. also the Baraita Yoma 71b on Shemayah and Abtalyon, which is paradigmatic: 'The multitude left the High Priest and followed Shemayah and Abtalyon' ואזלי בתר ש"ו ואי. See on the subject itself, R. Meyer, *Tradition und Neuschöpfung im Antiken Judentum*, BAL, 110, 2 (1965), 48ff., 63ff., and A. S. v.d. Woude, *Die messianische Vorstellung der Gemeinde von Qumran*, 1957, 239-242. On the charismatic element in early tannaitic Pharisaism, see below p.56 n.65.

stamp. First and foremost we would have to mention here Judas of Galilee who appeared in 6 A.D. along with the Pharisee Zadok and proclaimed the doctrine – probably for the sake of the 'Rule of God' – that no ruler should be recognized as sovereign save God alone. Thus Judas became the founder of the Zealot movement.[17] Luke's Gamaliel can say of him: 'he brought a crowd of the people after him (as supporters) (and) to their destruction' *(ἀπέστησεν λαὸν ὀπίσω αὐτοῦ).*[18] In addition Josephus gives account of a whole series of enthusiast messianic 'prophets', including among them the Egyptian and Theudas who are mentioned by Luke (Acts 5.36; 21.38) – each of whom persuaded some crowds of the people to follow them into the wilderness where they claimed that the wonders of the last days would be manifested. It may well be that behind this lay the idea of a Moses *redivivus* or of the messianic prophet of Deut 18.15ff.[19] In this connection we find the idea of 'following after' or even of 'leading on', occurring in an almost stereotype fashion – the enthusiast groups being in part unarmed.[20] Lk 21.8 also warns against false messiahs in a manner which is entirely in conformity with the reports of Josephus: 'do not follow after them' *(μὴ πορευθῆτε ὀπίσω αὐτῶν,* cf. Mt 24.26 and Jn 10.5).

Early rabbinic exegesis of Exodus might be referring in MekEx 14.15 to the way in which these apocalyptic prophets faithfully interpreted the second eschatological exodus along the lines of the first:

'others say: it is in accord with the faith with which they believed in me (כדי היא האמנה שהאמינו בי) that I should split the sea for them.' For they did not say to Moses: 'how can we go into the wilderness when there are no provisions in our hands for wandering' *but rather they believed and followed after Moses* (אלא האמינו והלכו אחרי משה).

[17] Josephus *Bell* 2.117-119, 433; 7.253; *Ant* 18.2-10, 23-25; 20.102; on this scale see also M. Hengel op.cit. (p.17 n.4), 79-150.

[18] Acts 5.37: E. Haenchen, *Apg* MeyerK 1965, 14th ed., 207 n.8 (E.T. *The Acts of the Apostles*, 1971, 253 n.8). 'Luke combines the Greek turn of phrase "bring the people to its downfall" with the biblical "lead a people after one".' The two do not of course have the same meaning, for the former interprets the latter negatively.

[19] See *Ant* 18.85-87: the messianic prophet in Samaria; *Ant* 20.97f.: Theudas; *Ant* 20.167 = *Bell* 2.259: anonymous 'prophets' under Felix; *Ant* 20.169-172 = *Bell* 2.261-263, cf. Acts 21.38 *(ἐξαγαγών)*: the Egyptian; *Ant* 20.188: an anonymous prophet under Festus. Cf. also *Bell* 7.437-441: the pseudo-prophet Jonathan in Cyrene, and Socrates, *Hist Eccl* 7.38 *(ἡγεῖτο... ἠκολούθουν)*: the Jewish pseudo-Messiah in Crete in the 5th century A.D. Cf. on the subject R. Meyer, op.cit. (p.17 n.6), 82-88 and ThW 6.826f. (E.T. 6.826f.), see also M. Hengel op.cit. 235ff. On *Moses redivivus*, see J. Jeremias, ThW 4.864-867 (E.T. 4.856ff.) and the rabbinical references quoted there, cf. also Bill 1.85f.: 2.284. On the desert as the place of eschatological salvation see M. Hengel, op.cit. 257ff.

[20] *Ant* 20, 97: ἔπεσθαι πρὸς τὸν Ἰορδάνην αὐτῷ...167: ἔπειθον αὐτοῖς εἰς τὴν ἐρημίαν ἔπεσθαι 188: ἔπεσθαι μέχρι τῆς ἐρημίας αὐτῷ... τοὺς ἀκολουθήσαντας... Bell 2.259: τὸ πλῆθος ἔπειθον καὶ προῆγον εἰς τὴν ἐρημίαν 261: ἀθροίζει τῶν ἠπατημένων περιαγαγὼν δὲ αὐτούς.7.438: οὐκ ὀλίγους τῶν ἀπόρων ἀνέπεισε προσέχειν αὐτῷ καὶ προήγαγεν εἰς τὴν ἔρημον σημεῖα καὶ φάσματα δείξειν ὑπισχνούμενος. On being unarmed see *Bell* 7.440. In the Gospels the term προάγειν occurs only in regard to Jesus' journey to Jerusalem to his passion in Mk 10.32, and to the return of the Risen Lord to Galilee, 14.28; 16.7.

The importance of this tradition becomes clear from the fact that in MekEx it is quoted in all three times. Closely linked to it is the idea of Moses as the charismatic leader: 'and he led Israel' (וַיַּסַּע = LXX ἤγαγεν Ex 15.22).

Here as well as 'following after' we also come up against other motifs which we encounter in the eschatological proclamation of Jesus: not being anxious, and wonder-working faith (Mt 6.25ff.; 17.20; cf. Lk 17.6 Q). In another passage this believing trust in the charismatic leader is identified with faith in God himself:

'this is to teach you that each one who believes in the Shepherd of Israel (i.e. Moses) (שכל המאמין ברועה ישראל: cf. John 10.1-16) is like unto him who believes in him who spoke and the world came into existence' (MekEx 14.31 Lauterbach 1.252.125ff.). The exegetical basis for this view was found in Ex 14.31: 'then the people feared the Lord and they believed in the Lord and in Moses his servant'. The reward for this faith is the redemption of Israel from Egypt (L. 1. 253.141ff.) and the gift of the Holy Spirit through whom they sang the song of Moses, Ex 15.1ff. (L. 1.252.132ff.).

Thus the 'demand for faith' corresponded to 'following after'. It may well be that the apocalyptic messianic prophets demanded the same faith in their message and person which Israel had once given to Moses when it went out from Egypt, which faith was equated with faith in the God of Israel. To believe in the messianic messenger thus meant believing in God himself and to follow that messenger meant following after God himself. A later rabbinical tradition directly relates faith and following to the Messiah and at the same time corrects the enthusiastic hope of an earlier age:[21]

After that the Messiah is revealed, leads Israel into the desert and is again hidden. 'Everyone who believes *on him* and *follows after* him and waits patiently, will *live* but everyone who does not believe in him but goes to the peoples of the world they will kill at the end': וכל שהוא מאמין לו והולך אחריו וממתין הוא חיה

Mt 24.23, 26, which is a parallel to Lk 21.8 quoted above, plainly warns against such false belief:

'if anyone then says to you: lo, here is the Christ or there, do not believe. . . . If they then say to you: lo, he is in the desert, do not go out; lo, he is in the (secret) chambers (ταμιείοις, cf. Is 26.20) do not believe.'

[21] Ed. Lauterbach 1.222, 82ff. //. MekEx 12.39, Lauterbach 1.110, 48ff.: 'they believed in him האמינו בו (= Moses) and followed Moses'. For the 3rd parallel see MekEx 15.22 (L. 2.84). On the whole subject see also Bill 3.198f. Part of the saying comes from Abtalyon (middle of first century B.C.) according to MekEx 14.15 (L.220.60f.). According to Ab 1.10 Abtalyon was a pupil of Simeon b. Shetaḥ.

It is very probable that, in Jesus' day in Palestine, not only the pupils of the rabbis who followed behind their teachers were linked with the idea of 'following after' but also the adherents of apocalyptic prophets or the partisans of the leaders of popular Zealot bands – men of the type of a Judas of Galilee or his sons, or that Eleazar ben Dinai of whom later rabbinical tradition said that he wanted 'to bring on the coming of the end by force'.[22a] Joining such apocalyptic 'prophets' or Zealot leaders of the people, some of whom made 'messianic' claims for themselves,[23] was conditional on אֱמוּנָה towards the message and divine authorisation of the 'charismatic' and a further concomitant requirement of 'following after him' was frequently a breach with one's own family and the renunciation of property and goods and indeed the utmost endangering of one's own life and martyrdom. In the concrete situation of their struggle concern for morals and piety diminished more and more just as there was little or no possibility of developing the intellectual play of casuistic legal scholarship.[24] Josephus says that the supporters of Judas looked with contempt on torture and death and spared neither relations nor friends when they were required to put into action what they recognized as the will of God. The outbreak of the Jewish war was for instance occasioned first and foremost by the fact that the Temple captain Eleazar, who was a son of the former High Priest Hananiah and belonged to the highest priestly nobility, went over to the side of the Zealots who a short while later murdered his father.[25]

Yet we must not think of these leaders, some of whom were more 'prophetic' in character, some more 'zealot-charismatic', only from the standpoint of an overcharged enthusiasm: the most successful of them, Judas the Galilean, and his son Menahem are expressly called σοφιστής by Josephus and this points to their being active also as 'teachers': especially in the case of Judas the element of popular preaching emerges clearly.[26] Much the same can be said of the last defendant of Masada,

---

[22] CantR 2.9 § 3, see also A. Schlatter, *Sprache und Heimat des 4. Evangelisten,* BFCTh 6, 4 (1902), 46, which also contains parallel passages.

[22a] see M. Hengel, op.cit. 129f., 356f.

[23] op.cit. 296-307 cf. also R. Meyer, *Der Prophet aus Galiläa,* 1940, 70-82.

[24] The radical features of renunciation of possessions or of the martyr ethic – emphasized by H. Braun, op.cit. (p.6 n.12) (see index 1.162 and 2.153, cf. also *Qumran und das NT,* 1966, 2.97f., 104, 117) – are also found in these movements: see M. Hengel op.cit. 233f., cf. below, p.59.

[25] *Ant* 18.23: ἐν ὀλίγῳ τίθενται καὶ συγγενῶν τιμωρίας καὶ φίλων . . . cf. *Bell* 2.409ff. and on this M. Hengel op.cit. 365ff.

[26] *Bell* 2.118: σοφιστὴς δεινότατος cf. 433, 445 and M. Hengel op.cit. 339 n.1 and 90f. We must not think of Judas and Menahem only as freedom fighters and leaders of armed bands but also as eschatological 'preachers of repentance', preaching in the tone of 'prophetic invective' (op.cit.94) cf. *Bell* 2.118: κακίζων, 433: ὀνειδίσας; cf. also ὀνειδίζειν in Mt 11.20. In *Ant* 17.152, 155, σοφισταί was the name given to the two teachers who zealously expressed their opposition to the presence of Herod's eagle in the Temple. On σοφιστής see also B. Gerhardsson, *Memory and Manuscript,* ASNU 22 (1961), 89, where attention is drawn to the parallels with the rabbinic scholars. The word appears as a foreign

Eleazar ben Ari, who was probably a nephew of Judas the Galilean and to whom Josephus attributes that heroic speech with the summons to mass-suicide: ταυθ' ἡμᾶς οἱ νόμοι κελεύουσι.[27] Furthermore the dividing lines between such figures and Pharisaism were fluid; notably the school of Shammai probably inclined towards the Jewish liberation movement (see below p.45f., 55f).

In a significant rabbinical tradition to which little attention has been paid we hear of Menahem and his 800 'pupils' (תַּלְמִידִים) who left Hillel equipped for battle; we also hear of the 'pupils' of the priestly Zealot leader Eleazar (ben Simon) who killed the (High Priest) Elḥanan (= Ananus son of Ananus) and drove out the Romans.[28] From this it can be seen that (1) the concept תַּלְמִיד (= μαθητής) was *not always* understood even in the rabbinic tradition itself in the strict sense as (the scholar's) *pupils*[29] and (2) that Pharisaism prior to 70 A.D. – and that means also in Jesus' day – had a left wing influenced by 'charismatic-eschatological' tendencies. We shall have to come back to this point.

Elijah is the most likely figure to have served as a prototype for these circles. Elijah, the אִישׁ אֱלֹהִים, was zealous for God's honour. His word had the power of fire and yet at the same time he was able to use the sword against the prophets of Baal and not only called Elisha to follow him but was also called upon to execute God's judgment on the dissident people (1 Kings 19.15-18). Among the people he was therefore identified with Phinehas.[29a] Practically *all* these Jewish groups shared the *zeal for the Law* which had revived in the Maccabaean period: the differences between them lay only in the way in which it was interpreted. The scholarly casuistic method of Pharisaism was perhaps the predominant one but it was by no means the only possibility. Judas the Galilean and his supporters concentrated above all on the first commandment: ' . . . thou shalt have no other gods (= lords) beside me',[30] whilst the eschatological prophets made the Exodus tradition the focus of their interpretation.

---

loan word in the Talmudic literature; see S. Krauss, *Griechische u. Lat. Lehnwörter,* 1964 reprint, 2.277f. On the transference of the term to Jesus, see R. Eisler, op.cit. (p.38 n.1), 1.53f.

[27] *Bell* 7.387 cf. generally 337-388 and Y. Yadin, *Masada,* 1967, 193ff. (English ed. p.193ff.).

[28] Text and explanation in S. Lieberman, *Greek in Jewish Palestine,* 1965, 2nd ed., 179-184 from Midrash Cant zuta; on Menahem cf. also jHag 77d and Babli 16b, cf. also M. Hengel op.cit. 365ff. Cf. also the rabbinical note which calls the (Zealot) Idumeans 'pupils' (תלמידים) of the school of Shammai, see Lieberman op.cit. 182f.

[29] For further examples of a completely unspecific use of תלמיד see in K. H. Rengstorf ThW 4.436, 30ff. (E.T. 4.416ff.) see TgO and TgJer I on Num 32.14.

[29a] On the school of Shammai see M. Hengel op.cit. 91, 204ff., 339f. On the Elijah tradition and Phineas see op.cit. 167-175.

[30] Op.cit. 95-114, especially 102f.

4 Charismatics and Followers in the Hellenistic world

These observations are supplemented by the fact that in the non-Jewish *Hellenistic world* 'following' and 'discipleship' can be found above all where the teacher was at the same time a *charismatic* in the sense of the θεῖος ἀνήρ – as in the Pythagoras tradition where for example it is reported – as a unique parallel to Mt 8.21 – that the rejected novices were treated like dead people and that a cenotaph was erected to them.[31] According to another legend an audience of over 2,000 was so gripped by *one* lecture that they did not return home but remained with Pythagoras – with their wives and children (Iamblich, *Vit Pyth* 6.30 cf. Porphyr 20). Empedocles, related to Pythogoras, gives an impressive picture of his own activity in his *Katharmoi* ('Purifications'):

'But I go about (among) you as an immortal God, no longer as a mortal, honoured by all. . . . When I come to them (?) into the busy towns, to men and women, I am honoured by them; however they follow after me *(ἕπονται)*, in their thousands, to learn where the path (leads) to gain, some requiring sayings from the oracle *(μαντοσυνέων)*, others seeking to experience a word that brings healing in their manifold sicknesses, having already long been riddled with severe pain.'[32]

The analogy in particular to the various redactional summary narratives *(Sammelberichte)*, say, in Mark, is manifest: 'there are few ancient witnesses . . . which come so close to the evangelists' accounts of the flocking of the masses to Jesus, the miraculous physician . . .'.[33] Both Pythagoras and Empedocles stand at the water-shed between the 'philosopher' and older type of the *'Theios Anthropos'* and *'Wundermann'* like an Aristeas, Abaris, Zalmoxis or Epimenides which was widespread in ancient Greece and, according to the investigations of K. Meuli and E. R. Dodds, may well have its roots in the influence of the north-Indogermanic shamans. F. M. Cornford plainly saw the early Greek philosophers as successors of the 'shamans', who embraced in their persons the original unity of seer, poet and wise man,[34] and it was still

[31] See B. L. v.d. Waerden, PW 24.220 (Iamblich, *vit Pyth* 17.73): μνῆμα δὲ αὐτοῖς ὡς νεκροῖς ἐχώννυτο . . . ἐκείνους δὲ ἔφασαν τεθνάναι. On the disciples of Pythagoras see also K. H. Rengstorf ThW 4.423f. (E.T. 4.421ff.), cf. H. Windisch, *Paulus und Christus* UNT 24 (1934), 59ff.

[32] Diels-Kranz, op.cit. (p.12 n.30) 1.354f., fr.B.112, and M. P. Nilsson, *Geschichte d. Griech. Rel.* 1955, 2nd ed., 1.744f. and H. Windisch op.cit. 63ff. On the characterization of Pythagoras and Empedocles see also M. Weber, *Wirtschaft u. Gesellschaft,* 1956, 1.351.

[33] Mk 1.21f., 39; 3.7-12; 6.12f., 53-56; cf. Acts 14.8ff. The quotation is from H. Windisch, op.cit. 64. On Empedocles, *Katharmoi* fr.132 and Mt 11.25-30, see T. Arvedson *Das Mysterium Christi*, 1937, 95.

[34] K. Meuli, 'Scythica', Hermes 70 (1935), 121-176, see above all 153ff.; E. R. Dodds, *The Greeks and the Irrational,* 1951, ch.v: The Greek shamans and the Origin of Puritanism,

possible for the Sophist Gorgias to say, when contemplating his own time as a pupil *(γενέσθαι μαθητήν)* under Empedocles: ὡς αὐτὸς παρείη τῷ 'Εμπεδοκλεῖ γοητεύοντι, in which connection it seems difficult for us today to understand how Empedocles could combine mantic prophecy, magic medicine and his rational explanation of the world.[35] Plato was above all the figure who brought together these diverse primitive features of the Θεῖος ἄνθρωπος and applied them to the philosopher. Appropriately his 'school' was also embued with an almost prophetic religious pathos which had the deepest influence on subsequent philosophical developments.[36] The Academy became the standard model on which later foundations of schools were based.

In the doctor Menecrates Zeus from the fourth century B.C. we find a remarkable and unusual peripheral figure among these 'divine' wonder-workers. He gave himself the name of Zeus and his followers, whom he had healed of the 'sacred sickness, obeyed him as slaves'. To certain of his followers *(ἠκολούθουν)* he gave divine names like Heracles, Hermes or Apollo and they constituted in a sense his θεῖος χορός.[37] The complete combination of a charismatic wandering teacher, a wonder worker and of a 'philosopher' endowed with supernatural powers appears later in the tradition about Apollonius of Tyana: those healed of demon possession become his pupils, the masses initially acclaim him but are repelled by his uncomfortable demands. Only a few real disciples share his life as a wanderer, full of deprivation as it was; and when he risks his life to go to Rome or Ethiopia all apart from eight or ten abandon him.[38] In this case

135-178; F. M. Cornford, *Principium Sapientiae*, 1952, 62ff., 88ff., 107ff.: ch. VII The Philosopher as Successor of the Seer-Poet, on Pythagoras, Heraclitus, Parmenides, Empedocles and Socrates. Cf. also M. P. Nilsson, op.cit. 615-620. A little later than Amos (7.15) the Boeotian shepherd, Hesiod, has his 'vision of a call' *(Theogon* 22ff.) – according to F. Pfister, RAC 4.971 'the two oldest visions reported by the recipients of the visions themselves' – and Parmenides begins his didactic poem with the description of a celestial journey with fiery, heavenly chariots and horses, reminiscent, among other things, of II Kings 2.11.

[35] See W. Burkert, RhMus 105 (1962), 48; according to Satyrus in Diog Laert 8.58/59. Empedocles is celebrated here also as ἰατρὸς... καὶ ῥήτωρ ἄριστος and as a weather magician and raiser of the dead.

[36] See on this H. Windisch, op.cit. (n.31), 27ff., on the θεῖος ἄνθρωπος in Plato; cf. also F. M. Cornford op.cit. passim.

[37] Athen 7.289 B and C; see O. Weinreich, *Menekrates Zeus und Salmoneus*, Tübinger Btr. z. Altertumswiss. 18 (1933), and above all here the synopsis of sources, 92f. However, his psychopathological evaluation is too one-sided, based as it is on modern criteria. H. Windisch is rightly critical of this op.cit. 68f., as is M. Nilsson, op.cit. 138f.

[38] Philostratus, *Vit Apoll* 1.16: the gaining of a closer group of disciples in Antioch: 1.17: his 'authoritative' teaching to the people *(ὡς νομοθέτης)*; 4.1ff.; the triumphal reception in Ionia and subsequent disappointments; 4.20: a man who is possessed becomes his 'imitator' *(καὶ ἐς τὰ 'Απολλωνίου ἤδη ἀπεδύσατο)*; 4.35-38: the discussion with his fearful disciples about the journey to Rome: 4.44: arrest and trial before Tigellinus (cf. in Bk 7 the similar events under Domitian ch.10, 12f., 31: the cowardice of his disciples); 5.43: the division among his disciples before his journey to Ethiopia; 6.12, 15: the adherence of Nilus the gymnosophist. The argument between Eusebius and Hierocles shows how there was later a

too the motif of 'following after' clearly comes to the forefront: his favourite disciple Damis – who according to Philostratos was the authority for the entire tradition about Apollonius and is most likely an invention of the author – asks his new master in Niniveh: 'Let us go, Apollonius, you *following after God*, myself following you!' (ἴωμεν... Ἀπολλώνιε, σὺ μὲν θεῷ ἑπόμενος, ἐγὼ δὲ σοί) (1.19). As against the traditional philosophers' schools 'theology appears as the core of his teaching and piety as the basis of his entire way of life'. On the other hand as a wonder-worker he is reviled by his opponents as a magician and a sorcerer and, among other things, the work of Philostratos is an apologia against such reproaches.[39]

Indeed according to L. Bieler the acquisition of individual gifted pupils and disciples was in general a favourite motif in the tradition of the θεῖοι ἄνδρες, taking its place alongside that of their attractiveness to the masses.[40] Clearly despite the difference in principle, which rests on the strict distinction between God and man in Israelite and Jewish tradition, indicated by the difference in designations, there do also exist between the θειοῖ ἄνδρες and the אִישׁ אֱלֹהִים in Israel, such as Elijah and Elisha, noteworthy points common to them both, of a phenomenological nature. Here among other things we have the reason why in the Hellenistic Roman period it was to some extent possible in Judaism for the great figures of the past and indeed even for some comtemporary groups, such as the Essenes, to be portrayed as θεῖοι ἄνδρες.[41]

5 'Calling' and 'Conversion' to Philosophy or to the Torah in the Greek world or among the Rabbis

The parallels for 'vocatio' from the Greek world constitute a special case. They occur pre-eminently where philosophy was laying a claim to truth, the character of which involved commitment in a religious way.

temptation to compare Apollonius with Jesus. Cf. also H. Windisch, op.cit. (p.25 n.31), 70ff.: on the situation as to sources see J. Hempel, *Untersuchungen zur Überlieferung von Apollonius von Tyana*, Btr. z. Religionswiss 4 (1920), *passim*, though he does indeed wrongly still hold to the idea of a Damis source; and F. Solmsen PW 20, 139ff.; on Apollonius and the Christian tradition, see K. Gross, RAC 1, 529ff.
[39] Quoted in J. Hempel op.cit. 49. On the motif of 'following after God' in the Greek world see H. Kosmala, ASTI 2 (1963), 38-85. On Apollonius as a 'magician' see *Vit Apoll* 8.7.2, 9, J. Hempel op.cit. 53f. and K. Gross, RAC 1.530f.: cf. the similar polemic against Jesus, below p.4 n.14.
[40] ΘΕΙΟΣ ANHP 1935, 1.123.
[41] See L. Bieler, op.cit. 2.1-36; H. Windisch, op.cit. (p.25 n.31), 89-114. On the fundamental point of difference as to the relations with God, see L. Bieler, op.cit. 2.24 (citn.) and H. Windisch, op.cit. 90f. On the stylization of the Essenes in relation to the concept of θεῖος ἄνηρ see my *Judentum und Hellenismus, Studien zu ihrer Begegnung unter besonderer Berücksichtigung Palästinas...*, Tübingen 1969, 1973², 453 (cf. E.T. *Judaism and Hellenism*, SCM, 1974, I. 247, II. 167.).

Thus for instance in the young Aristotle's fragmentary dialogue Nerinthos we already find three 'call-narratives': The Arcadian Axiothea after reading Plato's Republic hurried from her home to hear Plato and 'forgot from then on that she was a woman'. The Corinthian peasant Nerinthos read Plato's Gorgias, 'immediately left the fields and the vineyards, entrusted his soul to Plato and sowed Plato's (teachings) and planted them out' (αὐτίκα ἀφεὶς τὸν ἀγρὸν καὶ τὰς ἀμπέλους Πλάτωνι ὑπέθηκε τὴν ψυχὴν κὰι τὰ ἐκείνου ἐσπείρετο καὶ ἐφυτεύετο). Similarly we hear that the reading of Socrates' Apologia to Zenon of Kition 'took him away from Phoenicia' (ἐκ Φοινίκης ἤγαγεν).[42] One could take as a motto for these 'call-narratives' Augustine's description of his encounter with Cicero's Hortensius: 'Ille vero liber mutavit affectum meum... Amor autem sapientiae nomen graecum habet philosophiam, quo me accendebant illae litterae' (conf. 3.4.7f.). Still more impressive because it is almost a 'call to follow after' is the first encounter between Socrates and Xenophon (Diog Laert 2.48): Socrates stops him in a narrow alley, involves him in a conversation and finally asks; 'where do men become καλοὶ κἀγαθοί?' Upon the embarassed silence of the person thus asked, there follows the invitation 'follow (me) now... and learn (ἔπου τοίνυν... καὶ μάνθανε). And from then on he became a hearer of Socrates'.

This motif of a 'conversion to philosophy' comparable to a 'call' (see A. D. Nock, Conversion, 164-186) is to be found in particular in the early Academy and among the Cynics. Typical is perhaps the 'call' of the young Polemo who is said to have forced his way when drunk in to the lecture on σοφροσύνη by Xenocrates, the head of the Academy and to 'have been captured' by it after a short time (ἐθηράθη; for the image cf. Mk 1.17 ἁλεεῖς ἀνθρώπων see below p.76f. n.148/51), with the result that he attached himself to Xenocrates and became his successor as head of the Academy. In this it is above all the motif of radical freedom from the ties of possessions which stands out; it begins with Socrates' pupil Antisthenes who is said to have been the first to have contented himself with the meagre possessions of the later Cynic philosophers, stave, satchel and a single philosopher's cloak (cf. Mt 10.10 Q which goes beyond this rigorous position, and its attenuation in Mk 6.8f., see below p.75 n.146), with his pupil Diogenes who resolved to practice total poverty by reason of having watched a mouse (cf. Mt 6.26; 10.29f.) and with Crates, the pupil of Aristotle who was Zeno's teacher, who publicly declared himself

[42] Aristot. Fragments ed. V. Rose, 1886, 74 (= Themisius orat 33 p.356 Dindorf). On Zeno cf. the divergent parallel tradition in Diogenes Laertius 7.3 and the summons by the bookseller in regard to Crates, Zeno's future teacher, who comes along: τούτῳ παρακολούθησον. See on the other hand 9.21: Parmenides heard Zenocrates 'but followed not him', but Ameinias.

free of his enslavement to his property, using the appropriate form for the
emancipation of a slave (cf. Mt 6.24), turned his property into cash and
bestowed it on his fellow-citizens (cf. Mk 10.21) or according to another
tradition threw it into the sea and with his stick beat off his relations who
tried to restrain him from doing so.[43] In the case of Apollonius of Tyana
this renunciation of property is given an expressly religious basis cf. the
well known prayer ascribed to him: ὦ θεοί, δοίητε μοι μικρὰ ἔχειν καὶ
δεῖσθαι μηδενός.[44]

A further motif closely connected with the renunciation of property is
that of *breaking* with one's own *family*. Socrates had already been accused in these terms: 'the Master had made "his pupils obey him rather
than their fathers", relations and friends'[45] and the Stoic Musonius in the
first century A.D. points to the same conflict:

> 'Your father is a hindrance to you in philosophising; but the com-
> mon father of all men and gods, Zeus, admonishes and encourages
> you to do this. . . . Zeus' command enjoins man to be good which is
> identical with being a philosopher. . . .' Musonius continues to the
> effect that the use of violence on the part of the father must in the
> last resort remain without success, as he possesses no power over
> the capacity to think philosophically *(διάνοια)*.[46]

His pupil Epictetus depicts in unsurpassable manner the *freedom* of the
true Cynic philosopher from all ties, whether of property or family or
again of convention and custom:

> 'And how is it possible that a man who possesses nothing and who is
> naked, without house and hearth, untidy, without slaves and with-
> out a home town can live a happy life?' "Look at me I am without
> house, without home, without property without slaves! I sleep on
> the ground, I have no wife no children, no palace from which to rule
> but only the earth and sky and one rough coat. And what do I lack?
> Am I not without sorrow, am I not without fear, am I not free? . . .
> Who on seeing me will not consider that he is looking at his king and
> lord" '.[47] H. Hommel draws attention to a related passage: 'what is

---

[43] On Polemo see Diog Laert 4.16f. Parallels and literature in K. v. Fritz PW 21.2524. On
Antisthenes see Diog Laert 6.13; cf. also the saying in 6.6 related to Mk 2.17//; according to
Stobaeus, *Flor.* 3.462.14 this was ascribed to his pupil Diogenes, cf. also Dio Chrysostom
8.5; Jesus, of course, is not the 'physician' of fools but of sinners. On Diogenes, see Diog
Laert 6.22. On Krates, see *Elegy and Iambus,* ed. J. M. Edmonds, LCL 1931, 2.64: Diog
Laert 6.87f. and the deviant parallel tradition in Philostratus, *Vita Apoll* 1.13 cf. Stenzel PW
11.1625f. and A. Bigelmair RAC 1.706. Cf. also the example of his life companion
Hipparchia, Diog Laert 6.96f.
[44] *Vita Apoll* 1.33(34). Cf. also 1.13, 34(35): 2.40(41): 8.7, 11. The idea is an old one, cf.
Plato, *Apol* 23C: Socrates lived in the most extreme poverty 'for the sake of serving God': ἐν
πενίᾳ μυρίᾳ εἰμὶ διὰ τὴν τοῦ θεοῦ λατρείαν cf. Xenophon, *Memor* 1.2.1: 1.6.1-10.
[45] H. Hommel, op.cit. (p.12 n.35), 12f.
[46] Op.cit. 15 (Musonius 16 p.86f. ed. Hense). Quoted from H. Hommel, op.cit. 15.
[47] Epictetus, *Diss* 3.22.45-49.

morally good *(τὸ ἀγαθόν)* therefore has priority over any relation-
ships. My concern is not with my father but with the *ἀγαθόν* . . .'.[48]

Here we certainly have the nearest philosophical analogy to the sayings
about following in Q Mt 8.18-22 and Lk 9.57-62. Jesus too demands
complete freedom of the person who follows him; though of course on the
basis of an entirely different kind of reasoning and of a different ob-
jective.

All these cases centre on the notion of the clarity of philosophical truth
as that which transforms life. This quality of truth can itself be considered
'divine' just as can the person of the philosophical teacher or
of the θεῖος ἄνθρωπος – in accordance that is with the Greek 'predic-
ative idea of God.'[49] Yet though 'divine' it was at the same time
completely rational, demanding an ethical decision of men of true religious depth. However, what is missing is the concrete and personal
summons issued by the active God of history as he encounters men in his
freedom, and which gives to the calling of the Jewish prophets and
charismatics its unique stamp. According to the philosophical interpretation of the call, the θεῖος ἄνθρωπος, like the philosopher, follows the
divine nature or truth which lies within him: φημὶ τοὺς ἀγαθοὺς τῶν
ἀνθρώπων θεοῦ τι ἔχειν. This view which Philostratos puts into the
mouth of his Apollonius[50] is basically already to be found in a similar form
in Plato's Socrates, in Aristotle and above all in the Stoa, which regarded
the 'wise man' as without qualification 'divine'.[51] Thus for the philosopher – in contrast to the older views of the seer and wise man, whose gift
depended still on a special divine 'charisma' given only to them[52] – the
'truth' and the 'good' became available and teachable to those who strove
for it with all their might, just as in rabbinical Judaism the Torah itself as

[48] Op.cit. 11 (*Diss* 3.3.5 and the subsequent discussion). On 3.3.9 cf. say Lk 12.13f. H.
Hommel, op.cit. 22 further draws attention to the Democritus fragment 107 (Diels-Kranz
2.164), cf. on this, say, Mk 3.32-35. On the disparagement of possessions in Democritus see
Fragments 40, 77. Diels-Kranz 2.155, 160 and Diog Laert 9.35f., 39.

[49] See U. v. Wilamowitz-Moellendorf, *Der Glaube der Hellenen,* 3rd unaltered ed. 1959,
1.17ff. On the 'apotheosis' of human beings see also A. v. Harnack, *Dogmengeschichte,*
1909 4th ed., 1.138 n.1 and M. P. Nilsson, op.cit. (p.25 n.32), 1.184ff., 2.135ff.

[50] *Vita Apoll* 8.7.7 cf. 8.5, his answer to Domitian's question on why he was called 'God'
by men: ὅτι πᾶς . . . ἄνθρωπος ἀγαθὸς νομιζόμενος θεοῦ ἐπωνυμίᾳ τιμᾶται.

[51] On the equation of 'good' with 'divine' in Plato and Aristotle see H. Windisch, op.cit.
(p.25 n.31), 29ff. pointing to Mk 10.18 and 15.39. Cf., say, Aristotle, *Eth Nic* p.1177b, 26ff.:
ὁ δὲ τοιοῦτος ἂν εἴη βίος κρείττων ἢ κατ' ἄνθρωπον; οὐ γὰρ ᾗ ἄνθρωπός ἐστιν οὕτω
βιώσεται, ἀλλ' ᾗ θεῖόν τι ἐν αὐτῷ ὑπάρχει. On the idea of 'Theios' as the 'truly autonomous
man . . . free from every external law . . . because he himself carries the law within himself;'
see H. Windisch, op.cit. 32f. (Plato, *Laws* 875C) and on the philosopher see 33f. (*Republic,*
500 CD). On the Stoa, see op.cit. 42ff., cf. M. Pohlenz, *Die Stoa,* 1964, 3rd ed., 1.120ff.,
154ff., 199ff. On Epictetus see H. Windisch, op.cit. 48ff.: 'by training and restraint (one
can) become the drinking companion of the gods and, finally, share their power' (*Encheir*
15). Epictetus is of course very sparing in his use of the designation θεῖος for men.

[52] On the older view see H. Windisch, op.cit. 27ff. It has its after-effects later too,
especially in Plato, see F. M. Cornford, op.cit. (p.26 n.34), 62-87.

the only 'mediator of the revelation' of God offered itself to each Jew for the purpose of study and of the fulfilment of the commandments and at the same time 'was regarded as the essential good'.[53]

Even the view that man was created for the Law and indeed that it is – at least symbolically – 'implanted' in him was not alien to Palestinian Judaism. Thus according to TgJer I on Gen 1.27 man was created in the image of God from 248 members and 365 veins corresponding to the number of the Old Testament commands and prohibitions, giving the total number of 613 *mizwoth*. The analogous idea that man as a microcosm corresponds to the macrocosm is hinted at in TgJer I on Gen 2.7 where man is not created from normal earth but 'from the earth from the place of the sanctuary' (on Zion), from the four winds and a mixture of all the waters in the world.[54]

The 'calls' and 'conversions' of the philosophers can therefore be directly compared with those of rabbinical legends which described the troubles and sacrifices involved in the study of Torah, although in them as a rule the specific motif of a call and conversion is missing.

A typical example would be that of Hillel who, as a poor man, came from Babylonia and in order to study the Torah hired himself out as a day-labourer on a starvation wage, who in winter was snowed in whilst listening at the attic window of the school and almost froze to death overnight; thereupon Shemaya and Abtalyon, his teachers, judged that such a pupil was worth desecrating the Sabbath for.[55] Two divergent anecdotes are related about Eliezer b. Hyrcanus. According to the first he was almost dying of starvation when he began to study the Torah at the age of twenty-two because he received no support from his father. He was helped only as a result of the attentiveness of his teacher Johanan ben Zakkai. According to the second story his father first of all even wanted to disinherit him but when the wisdom of his son miraculously became manifest in the presence of Johanan ben Zakkai, the father made over to him his entire property and disinherited the other sons. There is also a report of the extreme poverty of Akiba who is supposed not to have begun his studies until the age of forty. He is also said to have been disinherited by his rich father-in-law

[53] See M. Hengel, op.cit. (p.27 n.41), 279ff. (E.T. 171ff.). Wisdom = Torah as the intermediary of revelation in Ben Sira; 231-236 on the 'ontological understanding of Torah' among the rabbis. On the Torah as the 'Good' see Bill 1.809 (Ab 6.3 etc.) and 3.238 (SDtn 11.17 § 43 with ref to Prov 4.2).

[54] For parallels see in Bill 1.901d and e; cf. also GenR 8.11 on 1.27: man is created out of elements of the upper and nether world.

[55] Yoma 35b Bar; cf. Soṭa 21a (the temptation of Hillel by his well-to-do merchant brother and God's intervention through a Bath Qol) with Cant 8.7. It may well be that Hillel had already begun to study in Babylon, see G. F. Moore, *Judaism* 1.77.

and finally to have been reconciled by reason of his success in study.[56] A description from a later period does indeed have the motif of call and conversion but in it we do not have the idea of sacrifice and the seriousness of the call to decision. On the contrary it is presented with true rabbinic wit as a picaresque tale. The robber captain Resh Laqish (mid 3rd cent. A.D.) falls on R. Joḥanan as he is bathing in the Jordan. R. Joḥanan, undismayed, demands: 'Your strength for the teaching of the law (לאורייתא)! The robber answered: Your comeliness for women (R. Joḥanan's comeliness was compared with Jacob's and the first man, Adam's). He replied: If you convert (הדרת), I shall give you my sister who is more comely than I am. The other agreed . . . rehearsed (הדר) the Scriptures and Mishnah and became a great man' (BM 84a).

The old and frequently repeated baraita Pes 49a/b:

'Let a man ever sell everything he possesses and marry the daughter of a scribe . . .' – should on no account be understood as a radical demand for the renunciation of possessions, but, as the context shows, has a dual purpose, of separating oneself from the 'people of the land' (עמיה־ארץ) and of conserving the teaching in one's own family.

In both rabbinic and Greek philosophical anecdotes of this type attention is focussed on personal attachment not so much to the teacher as to the teaching, whether Torah or philosophy. In both cases, one becomes a pupil in order to acquire 'wisdom'. K. H. Rengstorf, E. Bickermann and B. Gerhardsson have already drawn attention to further unmistakable connections between the rabbinical house of instruction and the Greek philosophers' schools.[57] However, the motifs of radical renunciation of property, transvaluation of values and the provocation of 'public opinion' for the sake of total freedom, which were typical of the early Academy, the Cynics and individual Stoics are not found in Rabbinic Judaism; basically there was an ability there to appreciate the value of possessions and of family[58] and the sole requirement for rich and poor alike was

---

[56] ARN Vs A c.6 ed. Schechter p. 30f., cf. also the picture in PRE c. 1 Bill 4.777. On Akiba see Schechter p. 28f.: See also above, p.14 n.36.

[57] K. H. Rengstorf, ThW 4.405f., 427f., 441f., and E. Bi(c)kerman(n), RB 59 (1952) 44-54; B. Gerhardsson, op.cit. 27ff., 45, 50ff., 60ff. etc. Cf. also M. Hengel, op.cit. (p.27 n.41) 148ff. (E.T. 78ff., especially 81).

[58] On the love of riches and their dangers see Bill 1.826f.; on the burden of poverty 822f. See also F. Hauck-W. Kasch, ThW 6.323f. On the 4th Commandment among the rabbis see above p.8 n.20. On the binding command to marry see Bill 2.372f. Cf. also 3.367ff. The only known unmarried teacher was the mystic, Simon b. Azzai, more a colleague than a disciple of R. Akiba's, who was also not ordained, see Bill 1.807 and above (p.55 n.63). Sometimes there was certainly a conflict of duties between study of the Law and the married state, see Keth 5.6 and the Gemara 61b-63a; cf. also Bill 3.371f. When BM 2.11 (see Bill 1.587 on Mt

simply to study the Torah.[59] The rabbinical school thus shows itself to be even more strongly 'institutionalised', but here we should note that our sources began to be committed to writing only from the end of the second century A.D. when the Rabbis had achieved unlimited authority within Judaism, at least in Palestine, Syria and Mesopotamia. Circumstances in Palestine might still have been substantially different in Jesus' day (see below pp.55f.)

The phenomena of 'following' and 'discipleship,' of being 'called' and of 'freedom from ties' were familiar both to Judaism and to the Hellenistic world, in their various manifestations – which in part were highly differentiated. It is possible for instance, that Mark, writing for Gentile Christians, has given more prominence to the merits of radical renunciation of property because he has them in mind, as his Hellenistic circle of readers was already familiar in a positive way with this, through analogous demands made by wandering Cynic or Stoic preachers;[60] while the Q-tradition perhaps placed greater emphasis on the breaking of family-ties which certainly was a particular stumbling-block in Palestine – as throughout the Orient – but which in Palestine was nevertheless in the forefront of men's minds through the apocalyptic tradition of an eschatological dissolution of family-ties, and because of the 'call to follow' issued by apocalyptic prophets and Zealot leaders.[61]

10.37) places the teacher above one's father, this corresponds to the claim attributed in Diog Laert 5.19 to Aristotle: 'Educators are to be more greatly venerated than those who merely produce, for while the latter bestow life the former bestow the morally good life', see H. Hommel, op.cit. (p.12 n.35) 16.

[59] ARN Vs A c. 6 ed. Schechter p.29 bottom and Yoma 35b Bar. See also below, p.51 n.50.

[60] Cf. the connection of ἀφιέναι and 'following after' in Mk 1.18// and 20 and 10.28, which may well be redactional, cf. A. Schulz, op.cit. (n.1), 117 n.101. Also Lk 14.33 could be stylized in a similar sense. Joseph and Aseneth 13 (ed. Batiffol p.57.3f.) shows that this motif of 'renouncing possessions' was known, as an expression of penitence, to the Hellenistic Jewish 'theology of Mission' of the Diaspora: ἰδοὺ πάντα τὰ τῆς γῆς ἀγαθὰ κατέλιπον καὶ πρός σε κατέφυγον cf. also 12 p.55.14f., the renunciation of riches and 56.12ff., repudiation by parents. It is therefore improbable that the ideal of poverty we find among Essenes and Therapeutai is meant (as M. Delcor RQ 5 (1966), 594 supposes). The whole thing is perhaps to be understood rather in the sense of the Jewish attitude of confession lying behind Heb 11.24-27. On the motif of 'abandoning' goods and possessions in philosophy, see above p.28f. nn.42, 43. It is to be found also outside the early Academy and the Cynics, say in Anaxagoras, Diogenes Laertius 2.7, cf. Plato, *Hippias major* 283 A and Philostratus, *Vita Apoll* 1.13; or even Lucretius, *Rer Nat* 3.1060f.: quam bene si videat iam *rebus* quisque *relictis* naturam primum studeat cognoscere rerum, see A. D. Nock, *Conversion*, 1933, 171f. and cf. in this connection the analogy in 2 Esd 13.4 which relates to study of the Torah (Violet GCS 18.400): 'Dereliquisti enim tua et circa mea vacasti et legem exquisisti'. See also Sextus Empiricus in W. Bauer, WBzNT, 5th ed., 61. (E.T. Arndt and Gingrich, p.125).

[61] See Mt 8.21f. and Lk 9.59-62; Mt 10.37 = Lk 14.26: See also above p.13ff. n.38-40.

6 Following, discipleship and charisma

What emerges, from this brief survey of both Judaism and the Greek world, is that 'following' and 'discipleship' and the radical demands and sacrifices connected with it are hardly to be found in the area of firmly established institutions. Rather, these ideas occur in contexts where the traditional order and its standards are repeatedly broken down, or indeed rejected outright. This can be seen most clearly in the apocalyptic prophets and popular Zealot leaders in Palestine and in the Cynic philosophers of the Hellenistic-Roman World. It is certainly not chance that when Josephus compares the Jewish parties with the Greek scholars and philosophers, the Pythagoreans are on a par with the Essenes, the Epicureans with the Sadducees and the Stoics with the Pharisees, so that there remain only the Cynics to be compared with the 'fourth sect of philosophers' (τετάρτη φιλοσοφία Ant 18.23) of Judas the Galilean – even if Josephus does not make this comparison explicit.[62] 'Following' and 'discipleship', 'vocation' and radical freedom from all ties develop precisely where old forms are disintegrating, and – as Max Weber already recognised, with his acute sensitivity to sociological contexts – they depend on the effects of the *charismatic* personality who breaks through the barriers of the commonplace, i.e. in the religious field they depend on the personality of the prophetic *teacher* and *redeemer* (bringer of salvation):

> 'Those who are the bearers of the charisma – the master and his disciples and followers – must, if they are to do justice to their mission, stand outside the ties of this world, outside the everyday vocations and also outside the everyday family duties.'[63]

Of course this charisma, being entirely related to particular individuals, can be transmitted only in a very limited way. 'Discipleship represents one of the most refined forms of the I-thou relationship and for this very reason is also something which involves small numbers and a brief timespan.'[64] The result of the subsequent formation of schools and traditions is to objectivise the free, charismatic effectiveness of the prophetic teacher and to diminish its power to offend its environment. 'Followers' and 'disciples' become 'guardians of the tradition' and 'members of the community' who feel bound by the 'canonical' inheritance from the master and strive to preserve this inheritance as definitely formulated 'teaching' for posterity. The free, prophetic *exousia* becomes increasingly petrified as the 'authority' of the head of a school or of an

---

[62] See *Ant* 18.11ff., cf. 13.171ff.; 15.371: Essenes and Pythagoreans; *Vita* 12: Pharisees and Stoics.

[63] Op.cit. (n.32), 2.834 cf. 1044. See also H. Windisch op.cit. (n.31) 22f.

[64] See P. Honigsheim. RGG 3rd ed., 3.1009f.

office-bearer, legitimated by virtue of the 'succession' (*diadochē*),[65]and in this way the living process of following the master becomes the formally defined *imitatio*.

7 John the Baptist and his Disciples

Of course within the many strands of this overall context what gives the Jewish *line of tradition* its incomparable depth and claim to truth is its conviction that the *one* God, the 'Lord of the World',[66] *bestows* this charisma – it is not an indwelling divine quality at one's disposal, as with the θεῖοι ἄνδρες and the Greek Philosophers – and that he *calls* the people to conversion through the mouths of his prophets and makes the individual *willing* to let himself be called and wholly to yield himself to the cause of the nearness of God's kingdom.

This linking of a call to repentance, which is both ethically and eschatologically defined, with the gathering of disciples in face of the judgment of God, as something directly imminent, appears with particular clarity in the case of a unique prophetic and apocalyptic figure with whom indeed Jesus had been closely associated before the start of his own ministry: *John the Baptist.*[67] It is of course true that we hardly know anything about how he gathered his disciples around him, but it may nevertheless be indicative that we hear nothing about his expounding scripture but only of his teaching his disciples special prayers[68] and of their having their own fasting practices, Mk 2.18. Nor did the circle of his disciples include all those he baptised; rather, according to the testimony of the Gospels and Josephus, he carried out his baptism of repentance on a great multitude of people who had been affected by his eschatological preaching of repentance. He did not wish to found another sect as such: his message was rather intended for all Israel. It may well be that the task of his disciples was not least to assist him when he baptised and preached to the people. His preaching was so successful that it finally prompted Herod Antipas to intervene, as he feared a popular revolt, 'for they seemed to follow his counsel in everything': καὶ τῶν ἄλλων (? thus MWE; ex corr A λαῶν, cf. Lat; conj. Niese ἀνθρώπων; conj. Eisler πολλῶν) συστρεφομένων, καὶ γὰρ ἤρθησαν ἐπὶ πλεῖστον τῇ ἀκροάσει τῶν λόγων, δείσας Ἡρῴδης τὸ

---

[65] This very general characterization could – with variations – be confirmed in the history of the most varied religious groups.

[66] On this popular Jewish description of God see G. Dalman, *Die Worte Jesu* 1930, 2nd ed., 267 (E.T. 325); Bill 2.176 on Lk 10.21b and 3.671f. on Heb 1.2; W. Foerster, ThW 3.1083 (E.T. 3.1084f.); cf. also M. Hengel, op.cit. (n.4), 99f.

[67] On Jesus' relation to the Baptist and his turning away from him, see E. Käsemann, EVuB 2.60, 99, 108ff. (E.T. 112ff.); cf. also H. Conzelmann, RGG 3rd ed., 3.641 (E.T. 68f.).

[68] Lk 11.1: κύριε, δίδαξον ἡμᾶς προσεύχεσθαι, καθὼς καὶ Ἰωάννης ἐδίδαξεν τοὺς μαθητὰς αὐτοῦ cf. 5.33. On fasting see Mk 2.18//s, cf. Mt 11.18//; See P. Vielhauer, RGG, 3rd ed., 807.

ἐπὶ τοσόνδε πιθανὸν αὐτοῦ τοῖς ἀνθρώποις μὴ ἐπὶ στάσει τινὶ φέροι, πάντα γὰρ ἐῴκεσαν συμβουλῇ τῇ ἐκείνου πράξοντες.[69] His message was an eschatological 'radicalisation of prophetical ideas'[70] and as the execution of the Baptist by Herod Antipas shows, it could be misunderstood in a political way. Even his clothing and ascetic diet should probably not be explained only by analogy with the Bedouins and the 'desert ideal'. Both the eschatologically motivated renunciation of possessions and the prototype of Elijah are relevant, the latter most likely being dominant and encompassing the eschatological motif.[71] The way the disciples of the Baptist, after their Master's death, developed into a messianic movement in competition with Christianity, and the identification of the Baptist in the Christian community with Elijah as the one who prepared the way for the Kingdom of God in terms of Mal 3.22ff. suggests 'that John understood himself not merely as the forerunner of the judge but alongside this as the mediator of salvation'.[72] Serious consideration should also be given

[69] *Ant* 18.118-119, cit.118. His influence on the common people must have been very great. According to Josephus 'the Jews' considered the defeat of Herod Antipas by the Nabataeans as a punishment for the execution of the Baptist.

[70] P. Vielhauer, op.cit. (n.68), 3.805.

[71] Against P. Vielhauer, 'Tracht und Speise Johannes des Täufers', *Aufsätze z. N.T.*, ThB 31 (1965), 47-54 and RGG, 3rd ed., 3.805. The ζώνη δερματίνη Mk 1.6// = IV Reg 1.8 LXX = *Ant* 9.22 corresponds to the Jewish interpretation of עוֹר אֵזוֹר (1 Kings 1.8) in the New Testament period, see Tg Jon in loc. דְמַשְׁכָא וְרְזָא and the application in Yalqut Shimeoni II § 224 to the ram's skin in Gen 22.13., cf. also T. Sheb 5.12ff. (p.452) and MQ14a = Hull 107b/108a: a leathern or skin belt is meant, worn over the clothing. A Jew who had but one set of clothes and the belt was held to be particularly poor; cf. S. Krauss, *Talmudische Archäologie*, 1910, 1.172f., 613f., n.611, 623, but perhaps even the ἐνδεδυμένος τρίχας καμήλου can be best explained in relation to Elijah's 'mantle': אַדֶּרֶת I Kings 19.13, 19; II Kings 2.8, 13f.; LXX μηλωτή sheepskin, pelt, see S. Krauss, *Lehnwörter* 2.335f. and Brocklemann, *Lex.Syr.* 383 talmudical and Syriac loan word: מילא or מילת = wool or woollen mantle, or ܬܲܟ݂ܣܵܐ tapetum, tegumentum; Jos *Ant* 8.353 ἱμάτιον; Tg Jon שׁוּשִׁיפָא , see on this Jastrow, *Dictionary* 2.1543 'a coarse cloak'. The 'garment of camel's hair was probably deduced by Gezara Shawa from 2 Kings 1.8 (בַּעַל שֵׂעָר) and the prophet's mantle Zech 13.4 (אַדֶּרֶת שֵׂעָר LXX δέρριν τριχίνην cf. Gen 25.25 M כְּאַדֶּרֶת שֵׂעָר). The capacity of Jewish exegesis for making combinations is shown e.g. in the explanation of כְּאַדֶּרֶת שֵׂעָר , in the case of Esau, in relation to the Roman emperor's *toga* GenR 63.8. This combination is also confirmed by the *varia lectio* δέρρην καμήλου (Cod D) and pellem (a). According to S. Krauss, *Archäologie* 1.138 'all woven materials from animals' could 'be included under the designation שׂער – except for sheep's wool'. The Baptist's clothing is then probably best to be regarded as an imitation of the prophet's garments in the O.T. and especially of Elijah, just as his criticism of Herod Antipas is linked to O.T. and prophetic prototypes, cf. Lev 18.15 and II Sam 12.1ff. On the Baptist as an ascetic see Mt 11.7f., 18 and Lk 7.25f., 33 and the in many respects parallel figure of Bannus in Jos, *Vita* II, whose pupil Josephus was for three years and who lived in the desert, used only garments 'from trees', used as food only τὴν αὐτομάτως φυομένην and frequently immersed himself πρὸς ἁγνείαν. Finally, Heb 11.37ff. shows that the Baptist's clothing pointed back to relatively widespread Jewish ideas of 'prophets' garments'. In that passage a stay in the wilderness, and rough garments of skins (μηλωταῖς and αἰγείοις δέρμασιν) are linked; in I Cl 17.1 the same garb is ascribed not only to Elijah and Elisha but also to Ezekiel, and indeed to all the prophets 'who' proclaimed 'the coming of the Christ'.

[72] P. Vielhauer, RGG, 3rd ed., 3.805; cf. R. Meyer, op.cit. (p.17 n.6), 89-99.

to the question which, on the basis of Jn 10.41 or Mk 6.14 respectively, is
answered positively by R. Bultmann (Joh, 11th ed. 300n.4. and Suppl.
Vol. 35 (E.T., 1971, 394n.4) and R. Meyer (*Prophet aus Galiläa,* 40, 102,
115) viz. whether miracles were not also attributed to John by his
disciples. When N. A. Dahl and G. Bornkamm therefore agree in emphasizing that the disciples of the Baptist represent 'the closest analogy' to
the disciples of Jesus,[73] we can fully agree – and in so doing we may
emphasize that in ancient Judaism it is precisely with the Baptist that the
prophetic and eschatological form of his activity finds its purest expression. It is clear then that the Baptist's disciples are much closer to those of
Jesus than the 'disciples of the Pharisees' Mt 22.16 or those of the scribes.
This is true without prejudice to the justified reservation made by G.
Bornkamm (l.c.) that 'even the circle of John's disciples (offers) no
adequate parallel to the special features of being "a disciple of Jesus".' To
find a definitive answer to this complicated question the peculiar character of Jesus' call to follow him must itself be examined.

[73] N. A. Dahl, *Das Volk Gottes,* unchanged reprint 1963, 161 and G. Bornkamm, JvN,
134. (E.T. 145) H. Braun, *Qumran u. d. N.T.* 2.1-25 rightly emphasizes that there are basic
differences between Essenism and the Baptist. By contrast, in *Zeit und Geschichte, Dankes-*
gabe an R. Bultmann, 1964, 97ff., H. Thyen underestimates the prophetic and charismatic
character of the Baptist as an eschatological preacher of repentance.

III. The charismatic and eschatological distinctiveness of Jesus' call to follow him

1 The 'misunderstanding' of the death of Jesus

Ever since Reimarus' day repeated attempts have been made to represent Jesus as a political revolutionary – I mention only R. Eisler, S. G. F. Brandon and Carmichael's recent *pastiche*.[1] Bearing in mind the kaleidescopic picture of the Palestine of that day, with its prophetic heralds and followers, its charismatic leaders and those they misled, we must make it absolutely clear that Jesus was neither a political messianic pretender nor an apocalyptic enthusiast and prophet like Theudas.[2] He is separated from the Zealot-apocalyptic forces of his day by a gulf which, overall, is hardly less profound than that which separates him from the Pharisees. He was however a man of his time, of his country, and of his people – a Jew from the Galilean 'people of the land' (עם האָרץ).[3] And just as we can discover a wealth of rabbinical parallels to the logia attributed to him by the tradition, so too we can assume the existence of parallels to those popular apocalyptic-zealot circles, of whose activities and views we have unfortunately only meagre traces in Josephus and in the rabbinical tradition. The first Jewish 'apocalypses', Daniel, I Enoch, Syrian Baruch and 2 Esdras by contrast come either from the second century B.C. – or like the Similitudes of Enoch (1 En 37-71) from the first third of the first

[1] On Reimarus see A. Schweitzer, *Gesch. d. Leben-Jesu-Forschung*, 1912, 2nd ed., 13-26 (E.T. *The Quest of the Historical Jesus*, 13-26) R. Eisler, *ΙΗΣΟΥΣ ΒΑΣΙΛΕΥΣ* 2 volumes, 1929f. Cf also: *The Messiah Jesus* 1931; S. G. F. Brandon, *The Fall of Jerusalem and the Christian Church*, 1951, and *Jesus and the Zealots*, ALUOS 2 (1961), 11-25; J. Carmichael, *The Death of Jesus*, 1961: there is no end to the attempts made in this direction, see now e.g. F. Pzillas, 'Der Messiaskönig Jesus' in: *Jesusbilder in theologischer Sicht*, ed. K. Deschner, 1966, 181-206. For criticism of these more or less highly imaginative efforts, which since R. Eisler are based above all on the interpolations in the Old Slavonic Josephus, see M. Hengel, op.cit. (n.4), 17f., 185f., 306f., 345ff., 385f.

[2] G. Bornkamm, JvN, 40 (E.T. 44) 'Jesus' message has nothing in common with these religious and political slogans'. However he rightly adds: 'The fact however, that such persons and their movements, and in considerable number, belonged to the history of that time helps us understand the suspicion cast on Jesus and his condemnation by the Romans'.

[3] See W. Bauer, *Jesus der Galiläer, Festgabe A. Jülicher*, 1927, 16-34, an essay of which the basic thesis still merits being specially heeded even today. See further E. Lohmeyer, *Galiläa u. Jerusalem*, FRLANT 52 (1936), 84ff. and O. Michel, 'Jesus der Jude', in: *Der historische Jesus u. der kerygmatische Christus*, ed. H. Ristow and K. Matthiae, 1960, 310-316. On the geography and sociology of Galilee at the time of Jesus, see A. Alt, *Kl. Schriften*, 1953, 2.436-455: according to this, local traditions about Jesus' activities are to be found above all in the purely Jewish parts of Galilee.

century B.C.[4] – or again from the period after 70 A.D. around the turn of the century. In both instances they are similarly remote from the time of Jesus and probably also from the Galilean milieu. The much debated question whether Jesus was an 'apocalyptic' may therefore not be answered simply in terms of these great apocalypses, which give evidence of considerable literary learning, nor in terms of his relation to the Essenes of Qumran; in the last resort it depends on the definition of the term.[5]

It remains beyond doubt that Jesus was crucified as a supposed messianic pretender. Further even if his condemnation by the Romans was based on 'misunderstanding'[6] there must nevertheless have been points of contact in his message and his activities, which made it possible for the misunderstanding to arise and which make the condemnation of Jesus and the *titulus* on the cross understandable.[7] Here there is much to be said for N. A. Dahl's suggestion: 'that the title of Messiah as an expression of false expectation was applied to Jesus as an accusation and as a term of abuse before it was accepted as a summary expression of the church's confession and proclamation after the appearances of the Risen Jesus'.[8] Thus the misunderstanding of which R. Bultmann speaks was primarily the misunderstanding of the Romans and then also – in another way again – of the people and the broader circle of Jesus' Galilean support-

---

[4] When we consider I Enoch 56.5f. this still remains the most probable period. Contrariwise Rome is not yet within the perspective of the author, see O. Eissfeldt, op.cit.(p.101 n.24) 839 (E.T. 619) and Charles AP 2.171.

[5] If with E. Käsemann we define apocalyptic primarily as 'expectation of an *imminent parousia*' (EVuB 2.105f., n.1) (E.T., 109 n.1) Jesus might also be called an 'apocalyptic'. Of course if the term is connected constitutively with the speculative description and computation of the events of the end, or with pictures of heaven and hell and the cultivation of encyclopaedic and scholarly apocalyptic tradition, he was not such. With G. Ebeling we may say that we have to 'distinguish between apocalyptic and apocalyptic', see ZThK 58 (1961), 235.

[6] See R. Bultmann, *Das Verhältnis der urchristlichen Christusbotschaft zum historischen Jesus*, SAH 1960, 3, 4th impression, 12: '. . . the death of a political criminal. It is not easy to understand this execution as the intrinsically necessary consequence of his activity; it took place rather because of a *misunderstanding* of his activity as something political' (my italics). We find a still more concrete statement in: *Die Erforschung* (p.6 n.12), 49: 'When he went into Jerusalem with his followers his appearance will have seemed politically dangerous to the procurator' (only to him?). On this one might ask: Did Jesus not have to reckon with such a possible 'misunderstanding' as he certainly was no starry-eyed enthusiast? Such a misunderstanding had also occurred between the Baptist and Herod Antipas: see above p.35f. On the subject itself, see E. Fuchs, *Zur Frage nach dem historischen Jesus, Ges. Aufsätze II*, 1960, 157f. (E.T. *Studies of the Historical Jesus*, 1964, 23f) and *Glaube und Erfahrung, Ges. Aufsätze III*, 1965, 18f. Cf. also O. Michel ThLZ 83 (1958), 164, O. Cullmann, *Der Staat im N.T.*, 1961, 2nd ed., 27ff. and R. Meyer, op.cit. (p.17 n.6), 17f., followed by E. Grässer, op.cit. (p.15 n.38), 26f., n.7.

[7] On the historicity of the *titulus* see E. Dinkler in *Zeit u. Geschichte, Dankesgabe an R. Bultmann*, 1964, 147f.: its formulation was 'deprecatory of the Jews and Roman in character' (148). Cf. also the comments by N. A. Dahl, which are methodologically significant, in 'Der gekreuzigte Messias', in H. Ristow and K. Matthiae, *Der historische Jesus und der kerygmatische Christus*, 1960, 157-169.   [8] Op.cit. 168.

ers.[9] I venture to doubt whether in any case one can speak of a real 'misunderstanding' where the Sadducean aristocrats are concerned, seeing they subsequently promoted the persecution under Herod Agrippa I and still later saw to the execution of James, the Lord's brother.[9a] For them it was probably a case of deliberate denunciation. There was a desire to be rid of the dangerous Galilean who was shaking both the foundations of Jewish community life and the order of temple-worship and the Torah (see below pp.70f.) It is only on the basis of the many strands of this complex set of circumstances that we can obtain a satisfactory explanation for the emergence of traditions – presumably of a polemical and Jewish cast – which linked Jesus with figures such as the founder of the Zealot movement, Judas the Galilean (possibly a messianic pretender) or the messianic pseudo-prophet Theudas. It is no accident that Luke puts such a tradition in the mouth of Gamaliel, the Pharisee, son of Hillel the Elder.[10] It may be that prior to its 'correction' by a Christian scribe, the much discussed Testimonium Flavianum also had a similar, pejorative character.[11] Both the Synoptic Gospels and the Gospel of John and Acts reflect involvement with this at least partially intentional 'misunderstanding'.[12]

This picture is supplemented by the reproaches that had been levelled against Jesus' exorcisms and healings from 'official' Jewish quarters, probably while he was still alive. These were to the effect that he was 'possessed' and was working as the agent and with the authority of the prince of all the demons[13] – a polemic which left its deposit in the later

[9] Cf. N. A. Dahl, *Das Volk Gottes*, new impression 1963, 161: 'actually it may well be that those who gathered round Jesus were regarded as a crowd of messianic Zealots not only by the opponents but even by disciples (cf. Mk 11.1ff.; 8.32f.; Lk 22.38; 24.21; Acts 1.6; Jn 6.15). They did not understand . . . Jesus' intention'.

[9a] In both cases the persecution was not directed against individual groups in the community but deliberately against its leaders.

[10] Acts 5.35ff; cf. Lk 23.5: ἀνασείει τὸν λαόν and Acts 21.38, the confusion of Paul with the Egyptian false prophet. We still find Celsus, who drew the material for his polemic largely from Jewish sources, – see M. Lods, RHPR 21 (1941), 1-33 – comparing Jesus with στρατηγός and λῄσταρχος, Origen *Contra Celsum* 2.12 (GCS ed. Koetschau 1.140).

[11] See *Ant* 18.63. It may be that the original text of Josephus was 'corrected' by a Christian editor even before Eusebius. On the other hand a complete forgery is improbable. For more recent literature see L. H. Feldman, *Studies in Judaica, Scholarship on Philo and Josephus (1937-1962)* n.d. 42b-43b; still basic is R. Eisler, op.cit. (p.38 n.1) 1.24-88; cf. also, in agreement, F. Scheidweiler, ZNW 45 (1954), 230-243.

[12] Here we have the cause of the tendency demonstrable particularly in the Passion Story, in all four Gospels, to exonerate the Roman authorities from responsibility for Jesus' death and to impute it to the Jewish authorities – a tendency recently exaggerated by P. Winter in the opposite direction (*On the Trial of Jesus*, 1961, esp. 112-135). Particularly on Mk cf. 12.13-17//s and 15.2-15; on Lk see H. Conzelmann, *Die Mitte der Zeit*, 1964, 5th ed., 78ff. (E.T. *The Theology of St Luke*, 1960, 90ff.); on John see 19.12; in 11.48 there are also echoes to be found of debates relating to this misunderstanding, see P. Winter, op.cit. 145ff. See also G. Lindeskog in *Abraham unser Vater, Festschrift for O. Michel*, AGSU 5 (1963), 325-336.

[13] This tradition also appears in Mark and Q, according to Mt also as a doublet: see Mk

Jewish assessment of Jesus as a sorcerer and seducer of the people. His disciples should also be included in this for the Talmudic literature also speaks, in similarly negative fashion, of his 'talmîdîm'. The key-word πλάνος[14] which in this connection occurs repeatedly in the most varied layers of tradition also goes back to Jewish sources. The martyrdom of James, the Lord's brother is a typical example of how the appraisal of Jesus is carried over to his disciples. According to Josephus, the High Priest Ananus (Ḥānān) – son of the Annas in the Passion Narrative – had him 'accused with a number (of his sect) as a lawbreaker and handed over for stoning' (ὡς παρανομησάντων κατηγορίαν ποιησάμενος παρέδωκε λευσθησομένους Ant 20.200), during the vacancy in the procuratorship following Festus' death. In the legendary account of Hegesippus James is killed, despite his good standing among the people, because, being himself seduced by Jesus, he called upon the masses likewise to let themselves be seduced by the latter (Eusebius h. e. 2.23.25: καὶ ἔκραξαν λέγοντες 'ὦ ὦ, καὶ ὁ δίκαιος ἐπλανήθη, cf. 12: ἐπεὶ ὁ λαὸς πλανᾶται ὀπίσω Ἰησοῦ; 10: ἐπλανήθη εἰς Ἰησοῦν; 11: περὶ Ἰησοῦν μὴ πλανᾶσθαι). This picture is supplemented by the Coptic text of a Gnostic

---

3.22-27; Mt 12.22-30, cf. also 9.34 and 10.25 and Lk 11.14-23. The reproach was possibly also justified by the fact that according to Mk 3.20f., Jesus was regarded by his own family as 'mentally disturbed' or 'possessed', see W. Grundmann, *Das Evangelium n. Mc*, ThHK, 2nd impression n.d. 81, followed by E. Haenchen, op.cit. (p.7 n.17), 139ff (E.T. 176ff.). Jn 7.20; 8.48f., 52; and 10.20f. also bear witness to this possibly widespread polemical tradition.

[14] For views of Jesus as a 'magus' and 'seducer of the people' in Judaism see the Bar Sanh 43a על שכישף והסית והדיח את ישראל Par Sanh 1076. The הסית points to the מסית in M. Sanh 7. 4a. Mt 27.63: ἐκεῖνος ὁ πλάνος; Jn 7.12 πλανᾷ τὸν ὄχλον cf. 7.47 καὶ ὑμεῖς πεπλάνησθε; Justin, dial 69.7: μάγον... καὶ λαοπλάνον and 108.2 Ἰησοῦ τινος Γαλιλαίου πλάνου; Origen, Contra Celsum 1.68 (GCS ed. Koetschau 1.22). 71 (124): θεομισοῦς... τινος καὶ μοχθηροῦ γοήτος, cf. also Eusebius Dem Ev 3.3.1-4 (GCS 23.108f. ed. I Heikel), Jesus as πλάνος and 3.6.1 (108) f.: μαγγανευτής τις ἦν καὶ φαρμακεύς, ἀπατεὼν καὶ γόης. It is reasonable to suppose that Gentile polemics took over these features from earlier Jewish polemics. On Jewish traditions about Jesus, see J. Klausner, *Jesus v. Nazareth*, 1952, 3rd ed., 17-55 (E.T. *Jesus of Nazareth*, 1929, 19-54) and M. Goldstein, *Jesus in Jewish Tradition*, 1950, 22, 27ff., 32ff. On the disciples of Jesus see again Sanh 43a Bar and AZ 16b/17a Bar, the conversation between Eliezer b. Hyrcanus and a 'disciple of Jesus' (see below p.46 n.30) and on Jewish Christianity the casting of a spell on Ḥanina the nephew of R. Joshua (around 100 AD) by the Jewish Christians of Capernaum, KohR 1, 8, see Bill 1.159. Generally A. v. Harnack, *Mission und Ausbreitung des Christentums*, 1924 4th ed., 1.169f. According to A. D. Nock in *The Beginnings of Christianity*, 5. 188, Lk was already rejecting the charge of magic; cf. also E. Haenchen, *Die Apostelgeschichte*, MeyerK, 1965, 14.347 (E.T. 404). There is a close connection between the rabbinical rejection of miracle as evidence for truth, as from the end of the first century AD, and the conflict with the Christians, see A. Guttmann, op.cit. (p.17 n.4), 386ff., 391ff., 405f. In the rabbinical formula אין מזכירין מעשה נסים we may see a rejection of the Christian 'signs of the apostle' (2 Cor 12.12, cf. Rom 15.8) – and parallel phenomena. According to J. Jeremias, *Abendmahlsworte Jesu*, 1967, 4th ed., 13 n.8 and 73 n.1, (E.T. 1966 p.19 n.7 and 79, n.1) the Jesus, 'hanged' (San 43a) on the 'eve of passover' for magic and seducing the people, was a disciple of Joshua b. Perahya (1st half of the first century BC). There is nevertheless hardly any doubt that the rabbis identified this figure with our Jesus. It is significant that this was possible. In Sanh 67a too (Ben Stada = Ben Pantera) there seems to be another transference of this kind.

Apocalypse of James, in which, with James' martyrdom in mind the 'seducer' motif is likewise the focus.[15] Thus it seems not unreasonable to conclude that in 62 A.D. the Sadducean hierarchy promoted the condemnation of the Lord's brother, who was a strict observer of the Law, using similar accusations to those with which they had promoted the trial of Jesus some thirty years earlier.

In similar defamatory fashion Josephus speaks of the enthusiastic messianic prophets and the Zealot leaders as 'seducers,' 'deceivers' and 'magicians' who 'under the pretext of divine revelation strove to promote riot and revolution (ὑπὸ προσχήματι θειασμοῦ νεωτερισμοὺς καὶ μεταβολὰς πραγματευόμενοι) and persuaded the people to go mad' (δαιμονᾶν τὸ πλῆθος ἔπειθον).[16] We must not overlook the fact that the four Gospels agree that the people and even Jesus' supporters considered him to be some kind of 'messianic prophet'.[17] Drawing all these points together, we will be bound to agree with J. Jeremias' judgment: 'Jesus was in the eyes of his opponents a false prophet' and as such was handed over to the Romans – emphasis being laid on his messianic claims. The various scenes of mockery in the Passion Narrative impressively illuminate this (Mk 14.65//s; 15.29ff.; 15.16-20//s and Lk 23.11): 'the mockery of the condemned travesties the charge of which he has been accused' (*Abendmahlsworte Jesu*, 1967, 4th ed., 73: E. T. *The Eucharistic Words of Jesus*, 1964, 79).

2 Jesus was not a 'rabbi'

From all this the conclusion may be drawn that to his contemporaries Jesus was not at all like a scribe of the rabbinical stamp. Consequently to use the term 'rabbi' to give anything like a precise characterization of Jesus is extremely misleading.[18] To be sure, Jesus was doubtless addressed as 'Rabbi,'[19] but around 30 A.D. this certainly did not mean the same

---

[15] See *Koptisch-gnostiche Apokalypsen*... ed. A. Böhlig and P. Labib. Special volume (3) of the Wiss. Zeitschr. d. M. Luther Univ. Halle-Wittenberg 1963, 84 Col 62 (55), line 7 cf. p.64 and A. Böhlig, NovTest 5 (1962), 207-213.

[16] *Bell* 2. 259: πλάνοι... ἄνθρωποι καὶ ἀπατεῶνες = *Ant* 20. 167 γόητες καὶ ἀπατεῶνες ἄνθρωποι, cf. also *Bell* 6.288; on γοής see *Ant* 20.160, 188; *Bell* 4.85; 5.317.

[17] Cf. Mk 6.14f.// 8.28// Mt 16.1; 21.11, 46; Lk 7.16, 39; 13.33; 24.19; see R. Meyer, op.cit. (p.17 n.6), 18ff., 103ff.; G. Friedrich ThW 6.842ff. (E.T. 6.828ff. esp 842ff.); F. Hahn, op.cit. (p.4 n.4), 380ff. with regard to Jesus as the 'eschatological prophet' see esp. 381 n.1 and 2. There is also a good survey in F. Gils, 'Jésus Prophète d'après les évang. synopt.', Orient et Bibl. Lov. 2 (1957), 9-30, on the Moses tradition 30-42.

[18] See above all R. Bultmann, *Jesus*, 1929, 55ff. (E.T. *Jesus and the Word*, 1958, 48ff.); *Geschichte d. synopt. Trad.*, 52 (E.T. 50); *Theol. d. NT.*, 18, 28 (E.T. 19.27): 'prophet and rabbi'. Even B. Gerhardsson, op.cit. (p.23 n.26), 326 n.4, who basically agrees with Bultmann on this point, adds: 'On the other hand Bultmann does not take sufficient account of the characteristics which distinguish Jesus from the Rabbis'. Cf. also G. Bornkamm, JvN 51, 88 (E.T. 57, 96).

[19] See F. Hahn's summary op.cit. 74ff. (E.T. 73ff.) ῥάββ(ε)ι is found only in Mk and Mt

as it did 100 or 200 years later; as yet it was not the established title of an ordained scribe. It may be that the original sense of the term corresponded to 'Sir', as a form of address to a higher-ranking dignitary, but the sense of 'teacher' is the connotation which most strongly established itself even though it could not competely eclipse the original broader meaning.[20]

An excellent example of this original linguistic usage is provided by the anonymous parable from MekEx 12.1 (Lauterbach 1. 7 11.82ff.) which is certainly old and relates to Jonah: A priest owned a slave who said 'I will run away to a burial place where my master (רבי) cannot follow me. But his master (רבו) said: I have Canaanite slaves like you (who can follow you and fetch you back)'. The term רב (= Master, lord): may thus also have been used for the 'masters' in Jesus' parables (see also below n.22).

___

as a form of address for Jesus in the Synoptic Gospels, see Mk 9.5 (//Mt 17.4: κύριε; Lk 9.33: ἐπιστάτα); Mk 11.21; 14.45 = Mt 26.49 where it occurs on the lips of Judas the betrayer. That Mt allows this form of address to appear only on Judas' lips, cf. further 26.25, and that according to him it is trenchantly dismissed by Jesus as a form of address for the community, means that there was a manifest polemic against the rabbinic 'constriction' of this title. In Mt even διδάσκαλε appears only on the lips of those who are not disciples, see G. Strecker, l.c. (p.4 n.4). On the other hand the plethora of forms of address mentioned in 23.7-10 indicates that even around 100 AD the form of address for scribes was in no sense uniform. It may be that the address διδάσκαλε and, along with it, ἐπιστάτα in Luke can be traced to an original 'rabbi' or 'rabbuni'. On the other hand the relatively frequent use of 'rabbi' in John is to be ascribed to a historicizing tendency. In 3.26 the title is also used automatically for John the Baptist. The form ῥαββουνί (vl ῥαββωνι Mk 10.51 and Jn 20.16) will, as a West-Aramaic equivalent of the targumic רבון (= M אֲדֹון), mean simply 'sir' (or 'lord'), cf. also Taan 3.8, Honi the Circle-drawer's address to God, acc. to Cod. Kaufmann, on which see P. Kahle, ThR NF 17 (1948/9), 212f. and E. J. Kutscher, Rocznik Oriental. 28 (1964), 45. It is probably not an 'intensive form' of 'rabbi', as F. Hahn, op.cit. 74 (E.T. 73), following G. Dalman, supposes. רב and רבן are, rather, originally interchangeable parallel forms like 'd and 'dn in the sense of 'lord' in Ugaritic (according to information kindly supplied by Dr P. Rüger).

[20] rb in Phoenician-Canaanitic and in Aramaic is an old, widespread and versatile form of address meaning 'highest one', 'great one' or 'lord' ('sir'), see C. F. Jean-J. Hoftijzer, Dictionnaire des Inscriptions Sémitiques de l'ouest, 1965, 271ff., c.f. Donner-Röllig, KAI 3.22f. and 42. The variant form rbn is found more rarely and only in the official Aramaic of the Persian Empire and in Palmyrenic, see Jean-Hoftijzer, op.cit. 273, cf. also the Nabataean inscription from Petra in M. Weippert, ZDPV 82 (1966), 297 1.5: rbnh = 'his lord'. Also Dan 2.14, 48; 4.6; 5.11 or the plural רברבי GenApoc 19.24. In the very numerous ossuary inscriptions in Jerusalem from the period before 70 A.D. rb occurs only once as a title, see Frey CIJ 2, 1218, and here again we have the indication of a calling: הספר CIJ 2, 1308; 12185.25 בר רבן ... is not clear – most likely it is a proper name, see 1110 (cf. Mk 15.7// s). On the other hand, 1403, 1410 and 1414 clearly belong to a substantially later period. There are three striking Greek inscriptions with διδάσκαλος 1266 (with Theodotion in hebr, Letters, cf. 1404), 1268, 1269. In contrast the title rabbi appears substantially more frequently in the later Jewish burials from the 2-4 centuries AD in Beth-Shearim, see 995, 1006, 1033, 1041, 1042, 1052, 1055; for further attestations from Palestine and the diaspora see in E. Lohse, ThW 6, 964 n.27 (E.T. 6.963 n.27). On the general meaning of 'rab(bi)' see G. Dalman, op.cit. (p.35 n.66), 274; E. Lohse, ThW 6.962f. (E.T. 6.961ff.); cf. Bill 1.917: 'in the NT "rabbi" is an honorific form of address = "my lord", "my master".'

Now we cannot easily decide whether in Jesus' day the connotation 'teacher' already predominated: in the Gospels κύριε appears as a form of address almost even more frequently than διδάσκαλε, and it is hard to say whether in individual cases what lay behind this was רַבּוּנִי,מָרִי or רַבִּי, the more so as in the tradition the form of address could be easily interchanged.[21] The interpretation of 'rabbi', as a form of address, given in Jn 1.38 doubtless reproduces the linguistic usage towards the end of the first century A.D. i.e. after the destruction of the Temple and the final victory of Pharisaism. At all events, in Jesus' day this form of address was not the preserve of the Pharisaic students of the Law.[22] In the eyes of his contemporaries, his supporters, and – negatively – also his opponents he seemed to be first and foremost an *eschatological charismatic* (to use the most all-embracing term possible) – as ἀνὴρ προφήτης δυνατὸς ἐν ἔργῳ καὶ λόγῳ with whom many linked the expectation ὅτι αὐτός ἐστιν ὁ μέλλων λυτροῦσθαι τὸν Ἰσραηλ.[23]

(a) To this it could be objected that Jesus was first and foremost a *teacher* who like the rabbis taught in parables and ingeniously contrived sayings, who spoke in the synagogue, gathered pupils around him, debated with his opponents and in so doing was able to use the Torah with amazing aptness.[24] But the counter-question can be put here just as well: By what right do we consider these features in Jesus' day as the exclusive preserve of rabbinic legal scholars? Is there not here a tacit presupposition of the circumstances of the end of the first or second century A.D. when Pharisaic rabbinism had won the final victory within Palestinian Judaism and excommunicated all deviating groups and teachers? We must not let our picture of Judaism in Jesus' day be one-sidedly prescribed for us by the one group which triumphed over all the others.

(b) However much the Pharisees may have promoted the development

---

[21] See G. Dalman, op.cit. 266-280 (E.T. 324-340): F. Hahn, op.cit. (p.4 n.4), 74-91 (E.T. 73-81).

[22] As an established title – despite the rabbinical tendency to date back the forms of their own period into the past – 'rabbi' only appears from the time of Johanan ben Zakkai and his disciples, i.e. very probably only after 70 AD. According to Ab 1.4-15 the five *Zugoth* up to Hillel and Shammai still did not bear it, and the designation 'rabban' for Gamaliel, Hillel's son, was still a particularly distinctive title of honour. Similarly ordination too became a fixed custom only after 70 AD and E. Lohse, *Die Ordination im Spätjudentum und im NT*, 1951, 33f. makes it too early. For further linguistic usage cf. e.g. T Sanh 4.4 (p.420), the form of address to kings אדונינו ורבינו or the Palestinian proverb jQid 60a.23, 38f. (Bill 1.971), and other contrasts between 'lord' (רב) and 'slave' (עבד) Ab 1.3; TBQ 11.2 (p.370); Gitt 22a/b, 37b and frequently. According to BM 84a Resh Laqish (died prior to 279 AD) said that as a 'robber' chief he had previously been called 'rabbi' and now was again so called in the rabbinic school.

[23] Lk 24.21. Cf. in Acts 7.22 the same formulation for Moses, and F. Hahn, op.cit. 389, 392(E.T. 377, 379f.) who stresses especially the influence of Moses typology in the community tradition (see also above p.21f.; cf. e.g. Acts 3.22 and 7.37. A. Schlatter, *Das Evangelium des Lc.*, 2nd unaltered impression, 1960, 458, draws attention to Judg 6.8 LXX: ἐξαπέστειλεν κύριος ἄνδρα προφήτην πρὸς τοὺς υἱούς Ἰσραηλ.

[24] Cf. e.g. R. Bultmann, *Jesus*, 56 (E.T. 48); G. Bornkamm, JvN, 51 (E.T. 56f.).

of the synagogue in Jewish Palestine and prepared the way for it, the synagogue was not an invention of the Pharisees and Scribes. First proofs for its existence are from the second half of the third century B.C. from Ptolemaic Egypt.[25] Intrinsically every Jew familiar with the Law was entitled to speak in it. Only after 70 A.D. – in connection with the exclusion of the mînîm – do limitations to this right become discernible.[26]

(c) Nor should the *prophet* and *teacher* be regarded in any sense as opposites. Indeed in the New Testament period if a 'prophet' wished to be more than a mere 'visionary', he had to be in a position to expound, with some degree of 'authority', the demands of the Law and the 'secrets' of the prophets, by virtue of divine inspiration and authority. This is true for Daniel in *Daniel* 9 as well as for the môreh haṣṣedeq;[27] nor are the various Essene, early Pharisaic (!) and Zealot 'prophets' any exception here.[28] If H. Braun coined the expression *Toraverschärfung* (intensification of the Law) for the Essenes and for Jesus' proclamation, there lay behind this in both cases the claim of an authoritative, charismatic and eschatological interpretation of the Torah. The Zealots may also be included here, while Pharisaism of the Hillel stamp – which was in the end victorious – went in the opposite direction (see below, n.68).

(d) Even the *controversies* between Jesus and the Scribes who opposed him can hardly be used to show that Jesus was a teacher taught in accordance with the Rabbinic method. Even could one point to individual analogies – e.g. the similarity of method in justifying the resurrection in Mk 12.27//s and in R. Gamaliel II Sanh 90b[29] – a closer comparison clearly shows the essential differences. In Jesus' case there is

[25] See the two inscriptions CIJ 2.1440 and Tcherikover-Fuks, CPJ 3.164 No. 1532a from the period of Ptolemy III Euergetes 246-221 BC and further W. Schrage, ThW 7.810f. (E.T. 7.810f.): cf. also M. Hengel ZNW 57 (1966), 174 n.97.

[26] Whether and in what way Pharisaism was dominant in the Galilean synagogues of the first half of the first century AD has not been absolutely clarified, see below, p.55 n.64: Reading the scriptures in the synagogue 'was something which, apart from some exceptions, everyone could in principle do', Bill 4.156. A similar situation prevailed for explanatory translation, reading from the prophets and preaching. It was a man's ability which was the decisive point, see 161ff., 171ff. and ZNW 55 (1964), 143-161. On Jesus' appearance in the synagogue see W. Schrage, ThW 7.830ff. (E.T. 7.831ff.). The later community, and in particular Luke, 'systematized' this feature, op.cit. 830 n.216, following H. Conzelmann, op.cit. (n.12), 177 (E.T. 180ff., cf. 223), see Lk 4.15f.; cf. Mk 3.1 and Jn 18.20.

[27] R. Meyer, ThW 6.821, 1ff (E.T. 6.812-828).

[28] A pure 'ecstatic' like Jesus son of Ananias, who repeated his warning in stereotyped fashion (Jos *Bell* 6.300-309), was an exception. And in this case his admonitions too exhibit rhythmical form and *parallelismus membrorum*. On the 'prophetical and charismatic' exegesis of scripture see O. Betz, *Offenbarung und Schriftforschung in der Qumransekte*, in WUNT 6 (1960), *passim*, and M. Hengel, *Zeloten* 242ff., and *Judentum und Hellenismus* (p.27 n.44), 416ff. (E.T. Judaism and Hellenism, 1973, I.228ff.). Cf. perhaps 1QpHab 2.8f.; 1QS 6.6f.: Jos *Bell* 2.136, 159. On the 'pharisaic prophets' see *Ant* 17.43-45: πρόγνωσιν δὲ ἐπεπίστευοντο ἐπιφοιτήσει τοῦ θεοῦ and the promise to the Eunuch Bagoas which may well link up with Is 56.4f. See further below p.56 n.65.

[29] See Bill 1.893, cf. O. Michel, l.c. (p.47 n.35).

no trace of the pernickety learnedness so typical of the rabbinical way of debating. The sole rabbinic tradition referring to a supposed exegetical *halakah* of Jesus on Deut 23.19 and Mic 1.7b, characteristically also attributes to Jesus its own inimitable mode of exegetical deduction, such that R. Eliezer b. Hyrcanus took pleasure in it.[30] As C. H. Dodd has already emphasized in his significant essay, 'Jesus as Teacher and Prophet', the majority of the controversies in fact were 'not simply ... within the field of legitimate discussion', but rather was there revealed in this conflict ... 'a radical divergence of religious principle'. Therefore – as Dodd likewise emphasizes – Jesus was taken by the leading circles of contemporary Judaism not as some kind of odd, 'fringe' teacher but quite simply as a seducer.[31] Despite the occasional use of exegetical argumentation by Jesus the basic inadequacy of the designation *'scribe'* for Jesus, is, finally, shown by the fact that the Old Testament is no longer the central focus of his message; and this distinguishes him both from the 'prophets' of his day and from the scribes. As a rule Jesus argues exegetically only when he is questioned or attacked by third parties about the Torah, and, in addition, also at times when his claims and authority are at stake,[32] and here it is often methodologically difficult to distinguish between Jesus' use of scripture and that of the Christian community, as the latter again was for apologetic reasons very much more interested in proofs from scripture.[33]

We do not find Jesus using the homiletic and haggadic midrash which played such an important part in the instruction of the later community.[34]

[30] THull 2.24 (p.503) and AZ 16b/17a. See also J. Klausner, op.cit. (n.14), 43f. (E.T. 38).

[31] C. H. Dodd, in *Mysterium Christi* ed. G. K. A. Bell and A. Deissmann, 1931, 72f.

[32] Cf. e.g. Mk 2.25-28//; 7.6-13; 10.1-12; 12.18-27, 35-37. Only 12.28-34 constitutes a truly exegetical 'teaching dialogue' in the positive sense. On the use of scripture in Q, see H. E. Tödt, *Der Menschensohn in der synoptischen Überlieferung*, 1963, 2nd ed., 243f. (E.T. *The Son of Man in the Synoptic Tradition*, 1965, 267ff.). Among the passages which 'relate to the presence of Jesus in the dominant group is *that which shows the contrast* which is evoked by his claim, his authority, his announcement of disaster to men, to the Pharisees, to the cities of Galilee and to Jerusalem'. (Hengel's italics.)

[33] R. Bultmann, *Synopt. Tradition*, 39-56(E.T. 39-54), goes into the 'form and history' of the controversies and emphasizes that there is the same kind of argumentation both in the rabbinical literature and in the controversies in the Synoptics (46, E.T. 45), but then he rightly adds that behind this there is a framework which is broader by far: the discussions of the rabbinical schools are 'for their part clearly influenced by the oriental mode of speaking and disputing and by primitive artistic means such as have been preserved and developed in the fairy tale (Märchen)' (47 E.T. 46). In all probability Essenes, Sadducees, Baptist groups, Zealots and apocalyptic prophets scarcely argued otherwise. Bultmann also rightly emphasizes 'that the formation of the material took place pre-eminently in the primitive Palestinian community' (49 E.T. 48). On the use of scripture in the Jesus tradition, see *Die Erforschung der synoptischen Evangelien*, 1966 5th ed., 31: 'because most of the sayings of Jesus which quote the Old Testament are open to the suspicion of originating in the theological debates of the primitive community'.

[34] The best paradigm for a 'homiletic-haggadic midrash', Lk 4.15-29, is however probably a composition of Luke's shaped in masterly fashion from relatively older traditions: cf., e.g., the speeches in Acts 2.14-36; 7; 13.15-47, etc. Passages in the Synoptics which are midrashic

It was the 'new content' and not the form, in Jesus' use of scripture, which was significant: The form he naturally shared with his age; the new content was not 'scribal' and 'rabbinic' but 'charismatic' and 'eschatological' in type. Already we find in it – at least partially – a developing 'christocentric understanding of the Old Testament, later characteristic of Paul'.[35] Also connected with this, however, was a sovereign liberty over against the letter of scripture, indeed over against the Mosaic Torah in general (see below, pp.69ff.). In his preaching Jesus was in fact not first and foremost an exegete: in addition he is innocent of the spirit of rabbinic learning. E. Käsemann clearly recognized this defect in the representation of Jesus as a 'rabbi learned in the scripture', by emphasizing that 'however this may be, the portrayal of the teacher of wisdom accords but ill with that of the rabbi, because the former lives by immediacy of contemplation, such as is familiar to us from the parables of Jesus, while the latter's existence is determined by meditation and by the bond which keeps him tied to scripture'. (EVuB 1.209) (E.T. 40-42).

(e) Traditions and forms usually attributed to 'wisdom' can already be found in the Old Testament prophets, for instance a complete 'parable' already confronts us in the mouth of Nathan the prophet in 2 Sam 12.1-5, and in Is 5.1-7 and 28.23-29 there are others which may have served as a prototype for individual parables of Jesus. Further, the ethical admonition had already been a constant basic element of prophetic preaching and the same is true of the proverb.[36] There are even stronger links between the teaching of the wisdom literature and the prophetic claims in the Judaism of the Hellenistic Roman period. Thus Ben Sira, the teacher of wisdom, used prophetic forms and compared himself to a prophet,[37] and in the 'David text' of the Psalms Scroll 11Q David is on the one hand called an enlightened 'wise man' and 'scribe' (חכם ואור כאור שמש וסופר), who nonetheless utters all his songs and hymns only through the 'clear and illuminated spirit' given by God and through 'prophetic inspiration'

---

in type, e.g. Lk 11.29-32 = Mt 12.38-42 Q or Mk 12.24-27// are of a markedly polemical character.

[35] O. Michel, *Paulus u. seine Bibel*, BFCTh 2. R. 18 (1929), 188, cf. 189: 'In Paul it is the charismatic understanding of scripture which corresponds to this prophetic scriptural testimonium'. T. W. Manson, *The Old Testament in the Teaching of Jesus*, BJRL 34 (1951), 312-332 fails to convince.

[36] This not least because of the many-sidedness of the basic term מָשָׁל, see O. Eissfeldt, *Der Maschal im AT*, BZAW 24 (1913) *passim*. According to him its oldest meaning is 'a popular proverb' (29). Cf. also *Einl. in das AT*, 1964, 3rd ed., 48f., 107f., 110ff. (E.T. 66, 82ff., 93ff.); Sellin-Fohrer, *Einl. in das AT*, 1965, 10th ed., 339ff.; C. Westermann, *Grundformen prophetischer Rede*, BEvTh 31 (1960), 144ff.; H. W. Wolff, *Amos geistige Heimat*, WMANT 18 (1964), *passim*, esp. 58f., 'Weisheit und Rechtsverkündigung' and 60f., the relations of Amos to 'ancient Israelite tribal wisdom'; J. Fichtner, 'Jesaja unter den Weisen' in *Gottes Weisheit, Ges. Stud. z. AT*, ATh II.3 (1965), 18-26.

[37] In regard to the prophetic genres in Ben-Sira, see W. Baumgartner, ZAW 34 (1914), 186-189: 'here we see an absolutely unique mixture of wisdom and prophecy' (186/7); see also M. Hengel, op.cit. (p.27 n.41), 246ff. (E.T.I. 134ff.).

כול אלה דבר בנבואה אשר נתן לו מלפני העליון).[38] The entire controversy
about the derivation of apocalyptic from prophecy or wisdom is basically
an idle one, because – in their opposition to the spirit of the Hellenistic
age – both had become inseparably bound up with each other.[39] It is
therefore only to be expected if we encounter self-contained parables
not, say, only as transmitted by the rabbis, but – alongside visionary
allegories – also in 2 Esdras (4.13-18,47-50; 5.51-54; 7.3-9; 8.41-44;
9.16f.). Even the Qumran Hymns (Ḥodayoth) develop their own linguistic imagery, though, of course, being esoteric, it is essentially different
from Jesus' parables. Jesus, by contrast, does not seek in apocalyptic
fashion to conceal his message by his parables, but – and here he is
comparable with the rabbis – first and foremost to explain, to argue out,
to convince. On the other hand, with him the parables never, in the
rabbinic fashion, serve the purpose of expounding the Torah, but are for
the explanation of his eschatological message.[40] Thus Jesus as a 'teacher'
using so-called 'wisdom' forms, and Jesus as an 'eschatological charismatic' or 'messianic' prophet, are in no sense contraries; the reverse is
true: each conditions the other, the unheard-of, revolutionary content of
Jesus' message sought the stamp and polish of an established form.

(f) The 'immediacy of his vision of life' which informs his preaching also
distinguishes Jesus from the rabbinical 'wise men' or 'sages'. For instance, according to Ab 3.7b, the motto of a certain R. Jakob (approx.
100 A.D.; according to other MSS Akiba or Simeon b. Johai[40a]) ran thus:

> 'He who walks along the road repeating (the Law) and interrupts his
> repetition and says: How lovely this tree is! How lovely this field is!
> to him it will be reckoned as if he had misused his life'

whereas by contrast, Jesus justifies his prophetic eschatological
demand – which is conditioned by the nearness of God – by the radiant

[38] See J. A. Sanders, *The Psalm Scroll of Qumran Cave II*, DJDJ IV (1965), 92 Col. 27.
2ff., 11; cf. also in The Psalm of Zion, op.cit., 88f. Col. 22.13f., the petition for prophetic
revelations, although the overall tenor of the apocryphal psalms has very much the charac-
ter of 'wisdom'. Col. 22.5/6 the $n^e b\hat{i}'\hat{i}m$ (of the past) and the $h^a s\hat{i}d\hat{i}m$ (of the present) are
equated.

[39] Cf. e.g. G. v. Rad, *Theologie des AT*, 1960 4th ed., 2.315-330 (E.T. *Old Testament
Theology*, 1965, 301-315), and O. Plöger, *Theokratie und Eschatologie*, WMANT 2 (1959),
passim; further M. Hengel, op.cit. (p.27 n.41), 374ff. (E.T. I.240-254).

[40] On this see, convincingly, C. H. Dodd, *The Parables of the Kingdom*, 2nd ed., 1961,
passim, though of course his wholly present 'realized eschatology' misrepresents the situation, and see also J. Jeremias, *Die Gleichnisse Jesu*, 1965, 7th ed., 17, 115f., 227 (E.T. *The
Parables of Jesus*, 1963, 16ff., 115ff., 226f.). 'They are all filled with... the certainty of
'inaugurated eschatology' (sich realisierende Eschatologie). Cf. E. Jüngel, *Paulus u. Jesus*,
HUTh 2 (1964) 2nd ed., 109f.

[40a] Cf. W. Bacher, *Die Agada der Tannaiten*, 1890, 2, 89 and the views of Ḥanina b.
Ḥakhinai Ab 3.4 and Ben Azzay ARN, c. 1 Vs. A. Schechter p.3 to the same effect, see
Bacher, op.cit. 1903 2nd ed., 1.435 and 414. The beauty of the world is 'vanity' (בְּטֵלה)
compared with the study of Torah.

beauty of the spring flowers and the boundless freedom of the birds under heaven[41] and *not* from the Torah. The nearness of the End is to be 'learned' *not* from apocalyptic calculations in the style of the book of Daniel but rather from the fig tree.[42] At the same time of course it can be seen that Jesus is also separated by a 'great gulf' from the traditional *prudence of the wisdom tradition*, which rests on the experiences of generations, since this prudence deduced something quite different from its directness of vision: 'Go to the ant, thou sluggard, consider her ways and be wise . . . which provideth her meat in the summer, and gathereth her food in the harvest . . .'.[43] The one-sided concept of a 'teacher of wisdom', which is too vague for Jesus' day, lets us grasp at best only a partial aspect of Jesus' preaching – and one which is basically only formal. Seen as a whole, his message cuts across every analogy, in terms of its content and its scope. Thus J. Jeremias is completely justified in opposing that 'tendency' – already setting in at an early date – 'which made of Jesus a teacher of wisdom and . . . had its greatest successes at the end of last century in Jülicher's exposition of the parables'.[44]

Thus, basically, Jesus stood outside *any discoverable uniform teaching tradition of Judaism*. It is not possible to assign him a place within the development of contemporary Jewish traditions. Nor can we learn anything certain about his training. It remains an undemonstrable supposition to suggest that he at any time attended a rabbinical school. Nor may the πῶς οὗτος γράμματα οἶδεν μὴ μεμαθηκώς of Jn 7.15, which may perhaps have its origins in Jewish polemic, be prematurely discounted, any more than τέκτων in Mk 6.3 as a description of his calling (rather than the attenuated *varia lectio, τοῦ τέκτονος ὁ υἱός*[45] &c., which

[41] Mt 6.25-34 = Lk 12.22-32; cf. Mt 10.29ff. = Lk 12.6f. Significantly, the motif of freedom from anxiety is to be found in Judaism in the exodus tradition of MekEx (see above p.22 n.21), which to my mind is under Zealot influence. Further rabbinical evidence is clearly later than Jesus, and is traced back to R. Meir (mid second century AD) or R. Simeon b. Eleazar (end of second century AD); they are directly related to Jesus' saying, so that the question arises whether pronouncements by Jesus may have not found their way into rabbinic tradition via Jewish Christianity; see the references in Bill 1.436f. (Qidd. 4.14//s etc.).

[42] Mk 13.28f. //s. J. Jeremias, op.cit. (n.40), 119f. (E.T. 119f.), sees in the parable not a reference to the imminent messianic woes, but to the age of salvation.

[43] Prov 6.6-11 cf. 30.25, see B. Gemser, *Sprüche Salomos*, HAT 1963 2nd ed., 39: 'the authors of the proverbs wage a constant war on laziness'.

[44] Op.cit. (n.40), 112.

[45] See above all H. Windisch, op.cit. (p.25 n.31), 120, 122-128. He makes Jesus a former disciple of the rabbis; similarly, but more guardedly, R. Bultmann, *Jesus*, 56 (E.T. 49). Jesus may have come from a Jewish family which was strict in its observance of the Law, but the view that Jesus himself – like Paul – was a follower of the Pharisaic approach, is hardly substantiated by the fact that later his brother James was a rigorist with good relations with the Pharisees (see *Ant* 20.201) or that those who were περὶ τοὺς νόμους ἀκριβεῖς were indignant at his execution by the High Priest Ananus, Son of Ananus. And, indeed, during Jesus' life-time, James had maintained an attitude of reserve towards him. On Jesus as a τέκτων see W. Bauer, *Wörterbuch z. NT*, 1958 5th ed., 1601. (E.T. Arndt and Gingrich, 816 s.v.).

is influenced by Mt 13.55), and his complete rejection in Nazareth.[45]
Jesus deliberately cut across the gap between the scribal theologian and
the ignorant עמי הארץ ('people of the earth'), a gap which was a distin-
guishing mark of Palestinian Judaism in his day, and, if we may so put it,
proclaimed the 'theological coming of age' of those who responded to his
message of the dawn of the Kingdom of God (Lk 10.21 = Mt 11.25). The
relatively numerous parallels to Jesus' sayings in the almost inexhaustible
ocean of ancient Jewish and rabbinical tradition can be explained on the
basis of the spiritual and mental milieu of his homeland and his age; for he
spoke as a Palestinian Jew to Palestinian Jews, and in such a way that the
ordinary people were able to hear and understand him. Consequently the
direct points of contacts between him and Pharisaism need not go beyond
what was in general the common property of the Judaism of the first
century A.D., with its commitment to the inheritance of the Hasidim of
the Maccabean age, and of Pharisaism.[46] The attempt to turn Jesus into a
'Pharisee of a special kind', repeatedly made, above all, in modern Jewish
portrayals of Jesus, is certainly helped on its way but in no sense justified
by the non-technical description of Jesus as a 'rabbi'.[47] G. Friedrich has
already brought out this point, in connection with his article προφήτης,
with a total clarity that is worth bearing in mind: 'There was between him
and the rabbis not a difference in degree as between two different
teachers, but a difference in principle. He taught as someone specially
authorized by God, so that his Word was God's Word, which men could
not evade.'[48] For reasons of clarity, therefore, we should desist altogether
from the description of Jesus as a 'rabbi'.

3 The rabbinic model does not explain 'following after' and 'discipleship'

Taking all these points of view into account, it becomes extremely improbable that the phenomenon which is of special interest to us –
'following after' and 'discipleship' – could be derived from the model of
the rabbinical scribes and the rabbinical school. There are no rabbinical
stories of 'calling' and 'following after' analogous to the pericopae in
Mark and Q, nor did the summons 'follow me' resound from any rabbini-

---

[46] See O. Michel, op.cit. (p.38 n.3), 312: 'He has contacts with Pharisaism only to the
extent that a common heritage deriving from Hasidism linked him with it'. On the Hasidim
as a movement of spiritual renewal for Judaism in the period of the Maccabean rising, see
M. Hengel, op.cit. (p.27 n.41) 319ff., 394ff. (E.T. 175ff., 218ff.).

[47] See the survey of the literature in H. F. Weiss, *Der Pharasäismus im Lichte . . . des NT*,
BAL 110, 2 (1965), 92ff. Cf. e.g. P. Winter, op.cit. (p.40 n.12), 133: 'Yet in historical
reality, Jesus was a Pharisee'. This frequent assertion can scarcely be refuted with R.
Bultmann's interpretation of Jesus as 'prophet and rabbi' (above p.42 n.18). On the
arguments against the older theses of J. Klausner see W. G. Kümmel, op.cit. (p.15 n.38),
2f., 188ff.

[48] ThW 6.844, 27ff. (E.T. 6.841ff.), cf. also W. G. Kümmel, op.cit. 1-14.

cal teacher in respect of entry into a teacher-pupil relationship. Whereas in the Gospel the decisive 'call' came from Jesus, entry into a rabbinical school was generally on the basis of an initiative on the part of a pupil.[49] Nor was this event ever described by the term 'following after' הלך אחרי – Aram. אזל בתר), but as a rule by 'learning Torah' (לָמַד תּוֹרָה[50]). It is significant that the New Testament equivalent *(μανθάνειν)* for this term which is extremely frequent in rabbinical sources appears only once in the Synoptics, namely in Mark, in an entirely different context – 'from the fig tree learn this parable' (Mk 13.28// Mt 24.32), and that we meet it only twice again in passages where there is considerable evidence of redactional activity in Mt (9.13; 11.29) where proofs from scripture and exegetical method again played a special part under the influence of a Jewish-Christian 'scribal school' (cf. Mt 13.52).[51] There is a *baraita* which can be placed not all that far away in time and place from the activity of Jesus, and which reproduces the typical course of entry into a rabbinical teacher-pupil relation. The Galilean and later wonder-worker Ḥanina ben Dosa came to 'Arab in Upper Galilee, 'to learn Torah with R. Johanan ben Zakkai' (שהלך ללמוד תורה אצל ר" יוחנן בן זכאי[52]). According to K. H. Rengstorf this 'use of למד in rabbinical Judaism gives evidence of a further strong intellectualising of Jewish piety as compared with the Old Testament' (ThW 4.405 E.T. 4.402). On the other hand, nothing of the sort can be found in any way in the preaching of Jesus – in contrast to Paul, the former Pharisee and scribe. Alongside the term in question there also appears that of 'serving'(שָׁמֵשׁ), as it was the duty of a rabbi's pupil to attend to his teacher – an idea which in Lk 22.26f. is clearly rejected for Jesus' disciples: ἐγὼ δὲ ἐν μέσῳ ὑμῶν εἰμι ὡς ὁ

[49] See K. H. Rengstorf, ThW 4.447 (E.T. 4.446ff.). Typical here is the call to attach oneself to a teacher, Ab 1.6b, cf. 1.4b. On the quite differently structured rabbinical anecdotes about entering on a training in the Law, see above p.31. Here a remote analogy may perhaps be offered in ARN Vs. B c. 26 p.54 Schechter, where Hillel at the gate of Jerusalem thus challenges the men who are going to work: 'Why do you not go away and inherit Torah and the life of this age and of the coming age? Thus did Hillel all the days of his life till he had brought them in under the protection of heaven.' Cf. the similar intention which Jethro had, in wishing to make proselytes of the Midianites, MekEx 18.27 (Lauterbach 2. 186 ll.108ff.). In both cases mastery of the Torah, not 'following after', is the subject.

[50] On the formula למד תורה see e.g. ARN Vs Ac. 6 p.29 Schechter: Akiba at 40 asks an elementary teacher: רבי למדני תורה p.30: R. Eliezer (ben Hyrcanus) was 22: ולא למד תורה; Yoma 35b: the rich Eliezer ben Ḥarsom was always intent on this ללמוד תורה(2x); Sanh 68a: The answer of the pupils of the mortally ill and excommunicate Eliezer ben Hyrcanus to their teacher's question, 'What have you come for?' was ללמוד תורה Cf. also Hillel's Aramaic rhyme in Ab 1.13. וּדְלָא יְלַף קְטָלָא חַיָב, cf. also Ab 2.12b, 14a, 16; 4.5a, 20; 6.3 and frequently. See also K. H. Rengstorf, ThW 4.403ff. (E.T. 4.402ff.) and below in n.55.

[51] On the 'scribal' tendency in Mt, see W. G. Kümmel (Feine-Behm), *Einleitung in das NT,* 1963, 12th ed., 65ff., 68f. (E.T. 1st ed., 78ff.). However, even in Mt 9.13 and 11.29 μανθάνειν does not mean rabbinical 'learning', see K. H. Rengstorf, ThW 4.408 (E.T. 406f.): 'This is what corresponds to the preaching of Jesus. His concern is not to impart information . . . but to awaken unconditional commitment to himself.'

[52] Ber 34b, on which see J. Neusner, *The life of Rabban Yohanan b. Zakkai,* 1962, 30f.

διακονῶν.[53] The term 'following after' is of course frequently used in the rabbinic sources in the sense of concretely 'walking behind the teacher' on journeys undertaken together, but there it is solely an expression of the natural subordination of the pupil, without any more profound sense, and is always connected with a real situation of wandering and travelling, so that it almost never takes the general meaning 'when I was a pupil with Rabbi N.N.'[54] Consequently the expression must on no account be over-

[53] See Bill 1.527, 920 and K. H. Rengstorf, ThW 4.437 (E.T. 4.436): Ab 6.5: Torah is acquired by 48 things: 1. 'by learning' (בתלמוד)... 9. 'by serving the wise' (בשמוש חכמים). Cf. against this the later tradition of R. Johanan (middle of third century AD) Ber 7b: 'serving the Torah (i.e. its teachers) is greater than acquiring it' and the justification on the basis of Elisha's behaviour 1 Kings 3.11; likewise the appeal to 1 Kings 19.21 in *Seder Eliyahu R* ed. Friedmann ch. 5 p.23. See also BB 10.8(b) and SNu 18.18 § 118 where 'serving the scholars' becomes identical with 'learning'. On Lk 22.26 cf. further Mk 10.41-45// Mt 20.24-28 and the anti-Pharisaic polemics of Mt 23.6-11. Cf. also E. Fascher, ThLZ 79 (1954), 331 on Jn 13.4-16: 'Where would a rabbi have accepted such an action?' In a rabbinical academy a strict hierarchy of superiors and subordinates was already necessary as a result of the progressive stages of training from scripture, Mischna, Gemara, independent decisions on *halakoth* through to ordination. Cf. on the other hand Mk 9.33-35 //s which brusquely rejects this thinking. In contrast to the rabbis Jesus was absolutely 'anti-hierarchal' in his attitude. On this see also the rabbinical self-appraisal in ch. 6 of *Pirqe Aboth* and the distaste for the 'ām hā 'āreṣ which we find in the strict application of the law, Bill 2.509-519.

[54] Above all, the difference in status is indicated – this is still so in the Orient today, see G. Kittel, ThW 1, 213 (E.T. 1.213): 'At no point do we detect any impulse towards giving this notion any fuller significance of making it a theological concept'. The term appears throughout in typically stylized anecdotes which report on a common way for teacher and pupil. In the Mishna there are not yet any such anecdotes; there are some few of them in the Tosefta and in the Tannaitic Midrashim; and they are relatively frequent in the Gemara of the later Talmuds: See TBer 1.4 (p.1); TPara 10.3 (p.638). In TPes 1.27 (p.157) = jAZ 40a, 42f. by contrast to the later parallels (Erub 64b and Lev R 37.3) there is still nothing said about the pupil's 'following' his master. Cf. also MekEx 31.12 (L 3.197) = Yoma 85a; SDtn 31.14 § 305 = Keth 66b; cf. also jHag 77a.53f. and ARN Vs A c. 4 p.21 Schechter; Ab 1.11 הבאים אחריכם does not mean 'going behind' but means that the pupils follow their teacher to where he has been exiled – abroad in pagan lands and there fall away from his teaching. The Aramaic phrase אזל בתר is, like the references in this later period generally, more frequent than the Hebrewהלך אחרי; Cf. Ber 23a/b, 24b (= RH 34b), 33b, 42b (in the funeral procession behind Rab's corpse); Ber 60a (2 traditions); Shab 12b (visiting the sick together). 112a (along with 'following' here we have the pupil's standing in front of the teacher, who is seated); BM 24b (2 traditions): Hull 48a/48b. The passages specifically explained by Bill 1.188 – e.g. Erub 30a (= Ber 44a and Keth 72b, both by Rabba b. Bar Hama (cf. Ber 23a/b; Shab 12b) in the sense of 'when I was a pupil with R.N.N.', taken in context mean only the same as all the others: 'When I was on the way with R.N.N. (as his pupil)'. 'Being a pupil' could therefore have a further special justification, see Hag 15a Bar: 'Ma'ªseh on "Acher" (the apostate), who was riding on a horse on one sabbath, and R. Meir (previously his pupil) followed behind him in order to learn Torah' (see above n.50). The basic difference from the Gospels lies also in the fact that it is always only the pupil, but never the teacher himself, who speaks of 'following after'. Occasional invitations to 'follow' have an entirely different meaning: 'Leave (your) *mishnayoth* and follow me (my interpretation)' שבוק מתניתין ואתי בתרי BQ 36b and Keritot 196. The institutional character of 'following' (walking behind) in the sense of a difference of status is indicated in MQ 16b: Mar Uqba, immersed in a legal case, forgets that he is not walking behind but in front of Shemuel, the president of the court, and for this he is one day excommunicated. This entire group of attitudes and ideas is *completely opposed* to Jesus' relationship with his disciples. In

interpreted. Moreover, this term does not reproduce the tendency, observable in the rabbinical teacher-pupil relationship, for the pupil to learn the *halakah* from the everyday behaviour of the teacher, even in its most intimate aspects, and moreover, this whole procedure has no correspondences in the Gospels.[55] For the communal life and table-fellowship which Jesus shared with his disciples did *not* mean that the disciples were to impress on themselves from Jesus' everyday behaviour their Master's *halakah,* and following after him did *not* mean imitating individual actions of his. It is singular what a small part basically is played in the Gospels by the 'example' or 'imitation' of Jesus: he seems to have directed his disciples' gaze not towards his everyday behaviour but towards the dawning *basileia* and the realisation of the will of God in its particular and specific requirements. Moreover, with him the learned atmosphere of the school, such as has been so impressively presented by Gerhardsson, is wholly lacking, with its stage-by-stage build-up of teaching, its refined memorising technique, and the years of intensive study, aimed at the pupil becoming himself a famous teacher, as, say, in the description of Akiba's unique career as a student: 'At forty he went to learn Torah, at the end of 13 years he taught Torah for the many' (בן ארבעים שנה הלךְללמוד תורה סוף שלש עשרה שנה לימד תורה ברבים).[56] Also the change of teachers occasionally recommended for the rabbinical student was unthinkable in following Jesus. In what he did, Jesus' aim was not to form tradition or to nurture exegetical or apocalyptic scholarship but to proclaim the nearness of God in word and deed, to call to repentance, and to proclaim the will of God understood radically in the light of the immenent rule of God, which indeed was already dawning in his activity; similarly, 'following after' him and 'discipleship' were orientated to this one great aim.[57] Whereas *stabilitas loci* in a fixed school building,

---

addition, it should be asked whether what the earliest anecdotes say about R. Johanan b. Zakkai have not, when all is said, been stylized only on the basis of the later established usage. At all events it will *not* be possible in general terms to derive the disciples' 'following after' Jesus from the rabbinical teacher-pupil relationship.

[55] Cf., say, in Ber 23a/b, the example of R. Johanan before his pupils who follow him, and the collection of anecdotes in 61b-62b, and the stereotyped replies of R. Akiba b. Azzai and R. Kahana to their shocked teachers: תורה היא ללמוד אני צריך.

[56] ARN Vs. A c. 6 p.29 Schechter; cf. on the other hand the well-known description of the regular course of training in Ab 5.21: 'with five years on scripture, ten on the Mishna, thirteen of fulfilling the Commandments and fifteen on teaching (לתלמוד)....' Cf. S. Krauss, *Talm. Archäol.* 3.218ff., 231ff. J. J. Vincent's suppositions in 'Did Jesus teach his Disciples to learn by Heart?' Studia Evangelica III, 2 TU 88 (1964), 105-118, are entirely on the wrong track.

[57] On changing one's teacher see S. Krauss, op.cit., 3.220. Cf. ARN Vs. A c. 3 Schechter p.16 – the advice of R. Meir, and, as a corrective, the warning against fragmentation, c. 8 p.36. On the formation of rabbinical traditions and schools, see K. H. Rengstorf, ThW 4, 438ff., cf. 452 (E.T. 4.435ff., cf. 453); see also W. G. Kümmel, 'Jesus und der jüdische Traditionsgedanke' in *HuG,* 15-35. On Jesus' demand for obedience, see Lk 6.46-49; Mk 4.2-9; Mt 21.28ff. and R. Deichgräber, ZNW 52 (1961) 119-122; See also below, pp. 71ff.

and an assured living were basic presuppositions for proper conduct of teaching,[58] Jesus went around in Galilee and the adjacent regions – more like a wandering Cynic preacher than a rabbi[59] – and spoke to the uneducated masses. He and his disciples quite likely lived on the strength of donations (Lk 8.3), and he rejected the making of any provision for the future. Consequently 'following after' has primarily the very concrete sense of following him *in his wanderings and sharing with him his uncertain and indeed perilous destiny,* and becoming his pupils only in a derivative sense. This is probably the original meaning of the much misunderstood saying about the homelessness of the Son of Man. Mt 8.20 = Lk 9.58.[60] The prior question in Mt 8.19 = Lk 9.57 (see above, p.19): ἀκολουθήσω σοι ὅπου ἐὰν ἀπέρχῃ grasps the intention of 'following after' Jesus absolutely correctly. But Jesus' answer intensifies it, showing in a figure that the way of the 'Son of Man' leads into total insecurity. It is in vain that we look for wandering rabbinical teachers who addressed themselves first and foremost to the עמי הארץ. J. Klausner's

---

[58] Already Sir 51.23 gives an invitation to his בית מדרש and in verse 29 to his ישיבה. The invitation in verses 23-30 is formulated in part similarly to Mt 11.28ff. except that there it is not wisdom (= Torah, Sir 24), but Jesus himself who is the focus of interest. On the relationship of the synagogue to the rabbinical school or academy, see M. Hengel, ZNW 57 (1966), 170f. n.91, cf. also B. Gerhardsson, *Memory* 85ff.

[59] On Jesus as a wandering preacher see already A. Bengel, *Gnomon* on Mt 8.23: 'habebat scholam ambulantem' ('he had a peripatetic school'), and also E. Haenchen, *Weg Jesu,* 33f.; O. Betz, op.cit. (p.1 n.2), 47 (E.T. 71): 'an itinerant teacher who was accompanied by a group of disciples. This does not necessarily indicate a rabbi'. H. Windisch, op.cit. (p.25 n.31), 157 points to the fact that the motif of the wandering teacher links Jesus and Paul and at the same time can be found in a θεῖος ἄνθρωπος in the manner of a Pythagoras or an Apollonius. Certain analogies between the wandering cynic teachers and Jesus are pointed out by C. Schneider, op.cit. (p.12 n.29), 1.35ff., 43f., 80 (and frequently), and by E. Wechssler, op.cit. (p.6 n.11), 242-266. Admittedly they overemphasize the points of contact. Cf. also E. Fascher, ThLZ 79 (1954), 331 and H. L. Jansen, RHPR 18 (1938), 242ff. The *Prayer of Nabonidus,* l.4 see R. Meyer, BAL 107.3 (1962), 16 and 30, Clearchus of Soloi according to Josephus *Contra Apionem* 1.176ff., Jos, *Ant* 8.46ff.; 20. 142; Acts 13.6 and 19.13 testify to the existence of wandering Jewish teachers, exorcists and wonder-workers in the Diaspora.

[60] See on this E. Schweizer, op.cit. (p.1 n.2), 13f. (E.T. 16) and *Neotestamentica,* 1963, 72; cf. also W. G. Kümmel, *Verheissung und Erfüllung,* AThANT 6 (1956 3rd ed.), 40 (E.T. 39). More clearly relevant than the parallel quoted since the time of Wettstein, in *Tib. Gracch.* 9 p.828c (see H. Almquist, *Plutarch u. das NT,* ASNU 15 (1946), 36f.) is the enumeration in Epictetus of the characteristics for the freedom of the true Cynic (*Diss.* 3. 22, 45ff.) – see above p.29 – although even this misses the concrete situation of Jesus. P. Vielhauer's objection (*Aufsätze z. N.T.,* 124) that Jesus lived in relative security – 'he had "his house" in Capernaum, he had friends and supporters who saw to his upkeep and gave him shelter' – misses the point that with the 'house' we have a typical datum for describing a situation, see R. Bultmann, *Syn. Trad.,* 257, 358 (E.T. 242, 332), and that Jesus, just like John the Baptist, really lived as a charismatic and eschatological 'prophet' in a tense situation in Palestine and actually in extreme insecurity and danger. This he gives expression to here by a figurative saying. If otherwise he says little about it, this is possibly because in Mt. 6.34 he was also referring to himself. His family's anxiety, consequently, is all the more plainly expressed in Mk 3.21. Cf. also the point made by O. Betz, Nov Test 6 (1963), 41f. regarding Lk 13.31-33.

assertion – that the 'wandering Galilean 'rabbi' and preacher' would, as עובר גלילאה, have been a 'commonplace phenomenon' – afterwards taken over by R. Otto and linked with the reference to Syrian prophets in Origen, c.Cels 7.9, will not bear closer examination.[61] Further, with Jesus one cannot detect any trace of the basic rabbinical injunction, always to seek fellowship and discussion with other scholars or individuals of like mind.[62] Preaching to the people in the open was exceptional among the rabbis, taking place say on feastdays or in funeral obsequies, but public teaching on the highway was – later at least – despised.[63] In general we must avoid overestimating the influence of Pharisaic scholars before 70 A.D. in Galilee, somewhat remote as it was in comparison with the major Jewish centres. In the seventeen years of R. Johanan ben Zakkai's activities in 'Arab in Galilee halfway between Nazareth and Capernaum – a period which according to J. Neusner is to be set between 25 and 45 A.D. – only two cases of *halakah* are said to have been put to him by the populace, in each instance relating to sanctification of the Sabbath. In this connection there was attributed to him the lamentation: 'Galilee, Galilee, thou abhorrest the Torah; thine end will be that thou fallest to the oppressors (i.e. to the Romans)' – hatred of the Law here meaning primarily contempt for the Pharisaic *paradosis* in accordance with the school of Hillel.[64]

However, should pre-70 A.D. Pharisaism (about which alas we know

[61] J. Klausner, *Jesus v. Nazareth,* 1952 3rd ed., 347 (E.T. 254f.) and R. Otto, *Reich Gottes und Menschensohn,* 3rd unaltered edition 1954 1f., cf. 267 (E.T. *The Kingdom of God and the Son of Man,* 1938, 13, cf. 315f.). The two late passages Hull 27b and Sanh 70a allude simply to someone passing through Galilee who displayed his learning in a (probably Babylonian) synagogue, probably at a time when Galilee constituted the real centre of Palestinian Judaism. Cf. e.g. also in Josephus, *Ant* 20.34 and 43: the missionary merchant Ananias and the legalistic Galilean, Eleazar, in Adiabene, or Akiba's sermon on fasting at Ginzaq in Media, see Bill 4.101. The parallel Shab 88a speaks only of a 'Galilean' who gave a baraita in the presence of the Babylonian R. Hisda (3rd century AD).

[62] See Ab 1.4b; 2.4b; 3.2b; 3.6 and above all 4.14. Cf. also the fate of R. Johanan b. Zakkai's favourite disciple, Eleazar ben Arakh, who went to Emmaus, where there was no academy, and became mentally atrophied from isolation, ARN Vs. A c.14 p.59 Schechter, Shab 147b; KohR 7.7, see J. Neusner op.cit. (n.52) 175 n.2; cf. W. Bacher, *Die Agada der Tannaiten,* 1903 2nd ed., 1.71f.

[63] On this see Bill 2.157 on Lk 5.1. According to MQ 16a (Bill 1.391) the patriarch Yehuda ha-naśi' forbade instruction of disciples in the street and excommunicated for thirty days R. Hiyya, who disobeyed. Cf. also Erub 29a: The fact that Simon b. Azzai (the mystic and ascetic, 100 AD see Hag 14b and T Yeb 8.4 p.250), who was never himself ordained, taught publicly in the street was still remembered in the 4th century by Raba as a peculiarity. On the public preaching of repentance on national fast days (in droughts, etc.), see Bill 4. 101ff., especially 104; cf. also Jos *Vita* 290ff.; on funeral sermons see Bill 4.585ff.

[64] See J. Neusner, op.cit. (n.52), 28f., cf. 31; R. Meyer, op.cit. (p.20 n.16), 70 n.1. 'Arab is the modern 'Arrāba (Arabic 'Arābet battof). On the whole question cf. already W. Bauer, op.cit. (n.3) 25ff. Against him H. Windisch op.cit. (p.25 n.31) 125f. drew attention to the legalistic Galilean Eleazar who, according to *Ant* 20.42ff., urged King Izates of Adiabene to be circumcised. Now, in Galilee, where the Zealot movement had its origins, there will certainly have been representatives of a rigorous legalism, but this is still no proof of the spread of scribal scholarship of a legalistic stamp like the Pharisaic *paradosis*.

much too little), and its teaching and training methods, have not as yet been so fixed institutionally and so completely fused with the scribal movement as it later was, and if it still possessed an essential charismatic component, then at least in some elements it was closer to the prophetic-eschatological movements we have described. The supposition that Pharisaism in its early period had a stronger eschatological and charismatic stamp than after the decisive catastrophes of 70 and 135 A.D. gains considerable support from the facts of Pharisaism's roots with the Essenes in the Ḥasidim of the Maccabean period, who were probably also the fathers of Jewish apocalyptic.[65] Nor, furthermore, is Pharisaism simply coterminous with the scribes, although they had always provided the leadership of the Pharisees and in time fused more and more with Pharisaism.[66] Pharisaism's total victory then also meant that it ceased to exist as a Jewish 'party': from around the beginning of the second century A.D. it is only a 'historical' term even in rabbinical tradition.[67] Probably in Jesus' day itself Pharisaism was not a uniform entity and was split into two wings one of which was more strongly universalist and intellectual and one which was more strongly national and eschatological: the mutually warring schools of Hillel and Shammai. Of course, only the Hillelites survived the catastrophe of 70 A.D.[68] This fact could explain why Jesus' relation to the Pharisees – once liberated from the oversimplified presentation of later tradition – seems not to have been entirely uniform. In this connection H. F. Weiss draws attention to Lk 7.36; 11.37 and 14.1, where the Pharisees warn him against Herod Antipas, Lk 13.31-32 and the 'Schulgespräch' (didactic discourse) in Mk 12.28-34, which was not turned into a controversy till Mt and Lk were written.[69] Perhaps Jesus initially gave the impression of standing to some extent with his message between the two 'sides'. Thus the Shammaite wing, which was probably rather stronger in Galilee, might to begin with have been relatively receptive to Jesus' call to repentance, while the humanity of Jesus' message had points of contact with certain formulations of Hillel's.[70]

[65] On this see above p.20 n.16 and p.45 n.28. Additionally see in R. Meyer, *Prophet* 56ff.; *Tradition* 55ff., 75ff.; ThW 6.819, 31ff; 824, 10ff (E.T. 6.816ff.; 823ff.); cf. M. Hengel, *Zeloten* 239 and on miracles among the early Tannaim, see A. Guttmann, op.cit. (p.17 n.4) 363-406. It may also be that behind the famous baraita Hag 14b on the 'heavenly journey' of Ben Azzai, Ben Zoma, Elisha b. Abuya and Akiba there could lie genuine ecstatic experiences and not just mystical speculations.

[66] See J. Jeremias, *Jerusalem z. Z. Jesu*, 1962, 3rd ed., 265-94 (E.T. *Jerusalem in the Time of Jesus*, 1967, 253ff. cf. 246 n.1, and 233-245) = II B 101-130 and R. Meyer op.cit. (p.20 n.16), 33ff., 43ff.

[67] R. Meyer, op.cit. 71ff, 84ff.

[68] Op.cit. 57, 73, 77, 85: Under Akiba's leadership the 'Zealot' wing again revived and supported Bar-Kochba. Cf. also M. Hengel, *Zeloten*, 91, 204ff., 295ff., 339f. and, on Akiba and Bar-Kochba, 245f.

[69] H. F. Weiss, *Der Pharisäismus im Lichte ... des NT*, BAL 110.2 (1965), 103f., 115ff.

[70] On Hillel cf. Ab 1.12f.; love of peace, love of humanity and humility; Shab 31a Bar: The golden rule as a summary of the Law, see Bill 1.357: Yom tob 16a Bar, Bill 1.421: See also above p.51. These are no more than casual points of contact.

However, Jesus' brusque condemnation of the παράδοσις τῶν πρεσβυτέρων (Mk 7.3, 5//s), which attacked the foundations of Pharisaism, and his deliberate, uninhibited approach to the עמ ה־ארץ was bound to lead to a radical breach. The circumstances in Palestine in Jesus' day are all in all too complicated and indeed almost self-contradictory, to allow us to present them schematically. To be specific, the later rabbinic sources, with their endeavour to project into the earlier period the sacrosanct institutions of their own time, require a thoroughly critical interpretation. Josephus can be of some assistance here, although he himself is a markedly tendentious author, who for example keeps almost completely silent about contemporary Jewish eschatology.[71] For this reason there can be no possibility of projecting on to Jesus and his disciples the teacher-pupil relationship of the later rabbis, as was done by A. Schulz and before him by B. Gerhardsson.[72]

4 Parallels and fundamental differences in relation to the phenomenon of apocalyptic-zealot prophecy

Particularly where Jesus' call to men to follow him is concerned, the fundamental parallels are more likely to be found in the direction of that *apocalyptic* and *Zealot prophecy* which we may assume retained a stronger hold in Galilee, which since Herod's day had been extremely disturbed politically, than did, say, Hillelite Pharisaism.[73] Here men could be called to 'follow after' their leaders very concretely and with a unconditional ultimacy. Those 'called' – and the term in the Qumran *War Scroll* and the *Damascus Document* means, significantly, the 'élite' of God[74] – had to be prepared, in the light of the proximity of the Kingdom of God, to leave family and possessions, in order to risk their own lives in unswerving loyalty towards, and complete trust in, the charismatic leader commissioned by God; this whether they were called to witness the wonders of the second Exodus in the desert as they followed the final 'redeemer'[75] or in guerilla warfare against the Roman occupying force and its Jewish accomplices to 'force an end' (see above, n.25),

[71] See M. Hengel, op.cit. 6-16.

[72] See B. Gerhardsson, *Memory* 326, referring to R. Bultmann, cf. *Coniectanea Neotestamentica* 20 (1964), 24, by way of qualification, 35: 'no ordinary Rabbi, much less a Rabbinic lawyer of late Tannaitic or Amoraic time'. Is the term 'rabbi' not used here 'inauthentically' and thus in such a way as to be open to misunderstanding? Cf. also on the whole question the criticism of Gerhardsson by J. Neusner HThR 59 (1966), 392, n.5.

[73] See M. Hengel, op.cit., 319-324, 333f., 337f., 353f., 375, 378f.; cf. 57ff. Lk 13.1 and Josephus' *Vita*.

[74] IQM 3.2; 4.10: קרואי אל.cf. 2, 7 = 1 QSa 2.2 and CD 2.11 and 4.4. The Old Testament prototype is Num 1.16 and 26.9.

[75] Cf. the rabbinic thesis: 'The final redeemer (the Messiah) will be like the first redeemer (Moses)', J. Jeremias, ThW 4.864, refs. n.140 (E.T. 4.860 n.140). See also H. M. Teeple, *The Mosaic Eschatological Prophet*, JBL Mon Ser 10 (1957), 49ff., 63ff. and above p.22 n.21 and p.42 n.17.

whose coming was dependent on man's co-operation with God. Thus too, for instance, the image of carrying the cross could come from a Zealot milieu, for by Jesus' day crucifixion had a centuries' old tradition behind it, and it is quite possible that more than *one* 'messianic prophet' was executed on the cross.[76] The Jewish interpretation of Deut 21.22f. seems to have undergone a decided transformation under the influence of the numerous crosses erected by the Romans in Jewish Palestine.[77] The *motifs* of 'renunciation of possessions'[78] 'exhortations to martyrdom'[79] and 'separation from family and dependants'[80] within Essenism and the Jesus tradition, which have been elaborated by H. Braun under the heading 'intensification of the Torah', were certainly also particularly evident

[76] See A. Schlatter, op.cit. (p.8 n.18), 350: M. Hengel, op.cit. 265f. and A. Schulz, op.cit. (p.1 n.1), 85. Thus according to Josephus, *Ant* 20.102, James and Simon the two sons of the 'messianic Pretender', Judas of Galilee, and (elder) brothers of the 'Pretender' Menahem, were taken prisoner and crucified by Tiberius Alexander, Philo's nephew, who was a Jewish renegade and at that time procurator in Judea. Cf. already the Rabbinical references to crucified 'robbers' and the crucifixion of Jose b. Joezer, the teacher of the Law, by Yakim-Alcimus, the High Priest, in the Maccabean period, see G. Dalman, op.cit. (p.7 n.15), 171f (E.T. 190); Josephus, *Ant* 13.380 and 4 QpNah 1.7 (Lohse 262) the crucifixion of 800 Pharisees by Alexander Jannaeus; *Bell* 2.73ff. = *Ant* 17.293ff. = *Ass Mos* 6.8ff. – the crucifixion of 2000 Jews around Jerusalem by Varus around 3 B.C. Cf. further *Bell* 2.241, 253; *Ant* 20.129, 161 the crucifixions by the procurators Quadratus and Felix and, *Bell* 2. 306, 308, by Florus. See E. Stauffer, *Jerusalem u. Rom*, 1957, 123-127. Probably crucifixion was used already under Antiochus IV Epiphanes: Josephus, *Ant* 12.256 and *Ass Mos* 8.1f.

[77] On the rabbinical exegesis of Deut 21.22ff. see Bill 1.1013, 1034 and 3.544. Cf. Targum Jer I Deut 21.23: 'For it is disrespectful to God to hang a man'(ארום קילותא קדם) אלהא למצלוב גבר) and S Deut 21.22 § 221 and the discussion in Sanh 46b together with R. Meir's parable. The rabbis then reduced the period of hanging, too, to a brief moment. The older – possibly pre-Roman – view is reproduced in connection with the Phinehas tradition by Targum Jer II on Num 25.4, when the Jews, probably under Persian Hellenistic influence, themselves crucified or impaled criminals (ויהון צלבין כל מן דמתחייב למתקטלא): cf. also Simeon b. Setah's procedure against 'the witches of Ascalon', Sanh 6.5c and jHag 78a 1.12. Significantly there is no mention in either example of any preliminary stoning. Perhaps we have here an early Pharisaic reaction under Queen Salome-Alexandra (76-67 BC), who was well-disposed to the Pharisees. In the later period under Roman rule, on the other hand, we find hanging only after preliminary stoning. While in Josephus, *Ant* 4.202 (and perhaps also 264f.) this lasts the whole day, its reduction to a moment is probably presupposed already in T Sanh 9.6 (p.429, 20f.). The discussion between R. Eliezer b. Hyrcanus in Sanh 6.5 and the sages, i.e. the majority of the teachers of Jamnia, shows the tension between older, rigorous views and the later teaching. The old baraita Sanh 46b ('should it be said "If a crime is committed you shall hang him" I would have said, "first hang and then kill afterwards, as the government (מלכות) does"; but rather it is said (Deut 21.22): "killed and hanged" – first let him be killed, afterwards let him be hanged') shows that crucifixion was discussed as a possible form of the death penalty but came to be rejected in reaction against the Roman custom, this being justified from Deut 21.22.

[78] H. Braun, *Radikalismus* (p.6 n.17) 1.73-80, 105f., cf. *Qumran u. d. N.T.*, 1.18 on Mt 6.19, 25; 21 on 10.9-12 and frequently.

[79] *Radikalismus* 1.100-108; *Qumran* 1.14 on Mt 5.10-12; see also M. Hengel, *Zeloten*, 261-277.

[80] *Radikalismus* 1.57 n.1; 95 n.2; the statements on the historicity of the individual traditions seem unfounded, see also above, p.13f.; further, *Qumran u. das NT*, 1.22 on Mt 10.34-39; 1.65 on Mk 3.31-35; 1.88 on Lk 9.59ff.

within groups of apocalyptic-enthusiastic and Zealot character.[81] Thus in the Palestinian Judaism of Jesus' day 'calling' and 'obedient following' appear to have had primarily a *charismatic* and *eschatological* basis.

Here too however the decisive differences from the message and activities of Jesus are at once evident. In contrast to the other eschatological movements of his age, and to their leaders, Jesus was not interested in placing himself at the head of an enthusiastic crowd. He rejected the popular demands for a sign.[82] What constituted the real and fatal threat to his work was the misunderstanding of his activity as political messiahship by the masses, who could not understand anyone proclaiming charismatically the nearness of the Rule of God without at least hidden political goals. Q's Temptation story in Mt 4.1-11// and Jn 6.14f. show that even later this was a matter for reflection.[83] As Jesus did not separate himself from the people with an esoteric group of the elect but continued to direct himself wholly towards the people in his preaching and his healing activity, he could not prevent the masses 'following after' him on this or that occasion; it may well be that the decision to arrest and execute him in Jerusalem was crucially influenced by the fact that the Galilean pilgrims at the Festival were well-disposed to Jesus and full of enthusiasm for him.[84] However, he himself never called the people as a whole to follow him nor made them his $\mu\alpha\theta\eta\tau\alpha\iota$, but always only select *individuals*; and this eliminates any interpretation of Jesus as a 'popular messianic leader' like Judas the Galilean or Theudas.[85] At least in the traditional form evidenced by Maccabeans, Essenes and Zealots, the idea of a Holy War was alien to him,[86] and the same is probably true of the idea that his activities and the activities of his disciples could 'force on' the eschaton;

[81] See M. Hengel, op.cit. 231-234; cf. 315ff. See also above p.23 n.24.

[82] Mk 8.11-13 = Mt 16.1-4 cf. 12.38f. = Lk 11.16, 29 also Lk 23.8f. and Jn 6.30. The proverb in Lk 4.23 should also be taken in this context.

[83] Mk 12.13-17 should also be understood from this standpoint. See also above p.39.

[84] On great multitudes 'following', see Mk 3.7//s; Mt 8.1; 12.15; 14.13 (= Lk 9.11, cf. Jn 6.2); 19.2 (= Mk 10.1); 20.29 (= Mk 10.46): cf. also Mk 11.8f.//s and generally the linguistic usage of $\check{o}\chi\lambda o\varsigma$ in the Synoptics; see on this R. Meyer, ThW 5.585ff (E.T. 5.586ff.). Even if all these passages except Mk 11.8 were probably redactional formations, they do produce an overall impression, and it can hardly be doubted that Jesus left a strong impression on the Galilean ᶜām hā'āreṣ, see e.g. Jn 7.48f., and on this R. Meyer, ThW 6.587-590 (E.T. 5.588ff.). W. Bauer's supposition op.cit. (p.38 n.3) 32, that 'the fact that people were not flocking to him in his own home area drove him up to Jerusalem', seems unfounded. The case could rather have been the opposite. Of course, to talk of 'flocking to him' does not automatically imply conversion and obedience (Mt 7.21 = Lk 6.46); on the contrary, the real danger for Jesus' activity lay precisely here, see above p.40 n.9.

[85] Although in the later tradition 'following' and 'believing', 'being a disciple' and 'belonging to the community' converge (see below p.62 n.97), the tradition nevertheless faithfully recorded that Jesus did call only on quite specific individuals and never on the crowd to 'follow' him. Even the sayings on 'following' him in Mt 10.37ff. = Lk 14.25-27, cf. also 14.28-33 and Mk 8.34//s, which have been stylized by the community tradition in a more general sense, show that Jesus' call was in this point capable of direction only towards individuals. Jesus' purpose did not lie in the development of a spectacular mass movement.

[86] On Jesus' situation as one of struggle, see O. Betz, NovTest 2 (1957), 116-137; H.

this would come only through the miracle worked by God: αὐτομάτη ἡ γῆ καρποφορεῖ.[87] His eschatological struggle was directed against the demonic powers in the light of the sicknesses caused by them, a problem the over-developed contemporary doctrine of retribution had solved far too simplistically by means of the equation that 'sickness is just punishment'.[88] His only weapon in this struggle was the *word of authority*, and from the start any use of violence was excluded, as can be seen from his bringing together the commands of the Torah in the dual command to love. It is certainly no accident that the term 'zeal' does not occur in the Synoptic Gospels.[89] He repulses his disciples most stringently when, following the example of the zealous Elijah, they wish to punish the inhospitable Samaritan village (Lk 9.51-56). Quite apart from the fact that no really telling reasons can be brought against the historicity of such an episode, the question of historicity is in this context secondary, as we can start from the position 'that the community created such scenes in the spirit of Jesus'.[90]

On the other hand, although he called only individuals, he did not, like the 'Teacher of Righteousness', found a community of the 'holy remnant' sealed off from the outside world, but remained open for all Israel. In particular he saw himself as sent to the 'lost sheep' (Mt 10.6, cf. 18.12f. and Lk 15.3ff.), the pariahs among the people, the taxgatherers, the prostitutes and the sinners, who were, equally, despised and hated by the Pharisees and the Zealots. The instituting of the Twelve itself, who included Matthew the taxgatherer and Simon, the 'man of zeal' and who cannot have been at all identical with the number of disciples called by him (the circle of which will rather have been larger – cf. Mk 10.32; 4.10 and Lk 6.13), points to this openness for all Israel, and has its prototype in certain charismatic and prophetic actions in the Old Testament.[91]

Braun allows only a qualified place for it in *Qumran und das NT*, 1.27, 49; 2.92 and frequently. He considers the idea of the 'holy war' in Jesus himself to be wrong but on the other hand accepts the idea of 'dualism' in relation to his 'struggle' (1.27).

[87] Mk 4.28; cf. J. Jeremias, op.cit. (n.40), 151f. (E.T. 151f.) and E. Grässer, op.cit. (p.15 n.38), 61: 'The βασιλεία τοῦ θεοῦ is not something growing within history but is the miracle which is independent of all human activity'. See also R. Bultmann, *Theologie*, 6(E.T. 5f.). On the Zealot precipitation of the end, see M. Hengel, *Zeloten*, 127-132.

[88] On Jesus' struggle against the demonic powers, see J. M. Robinson, *Das Geschichtsverständnis des Markusevangeliums*, ATh ANT 30 (1956), 34-75 (cf English equivalent, *The Problem of History in Mark*, 1957, 33-42), cf. also G. Bornkamm, JvN 61f. (E.T. 68) Mk does emphasize this point strongly, but it is also unmistakably present in Q and Jesus' activity cannot be conceived without it, see below p.64f. On illness as merited punishment, see Bill 2.194-197; 527ff. Its relative however was sick visiting as a work of love, Bill 4.573ff. On the significance of healings (and exorcisms – in ancient thought the two were not to be separated), see R. and M. Hengel, *Medicus Viator, Festschrift R. Siebeck*, 1959, 331-360.

[89] See M. Hengel, *Zeloten*, 185f. Jn 2.17 is the first to apply the idea of zeal to Jesus, in the reflective quotation from Ps 69.10 in connection with the cleansing of the Temple. Cf. also in H. Braun, *Radikalismus*, 2.57ff. n.1, the contrast with Qumran.

[90] R. Bultmann, *Synoptische Tradition*, 57 (E.T. 54).

[91] On this see W. G. Kümmel, 'Kirchenbegriff u. Geschichtsbewusstsein i.d. Urgde. u. b.

5 Jesus' call to 'follow' him applies only to the individual who is called

'Following' Jesus concretely as his μαθητής, as one called quite person- ally by him, and the related abandonment of family and possessions, cannot therefore have been the condition of participation in the ap- proaching Kingdom of God for all. It applied only to those individuals invited to 'follow' him in specific situations (cf. Mk 10.17-22//s).[92] It was not from everyone who heard him that Jesus demanded this unique attachment to his person and his way, the expression of which attachment was 'following after' him. Indeed, according to the Synoptic Gospels he did not first and foremost proclaim himself as the divine revealer but rather proclaimed the Kingdom of God as dawning with his activities. By contrast however, in view of the coming of the Kingdom *all* were com- manded to *repent* i.e. to acknowledge their own wickedness and guilt and to fulfill the gracious will of God; to do deeds of mercy and love, renouncing all self-glory and all pious claims on their Father in Heaven, and to will unconditionally to practise forgiveness of their neighbour, in response to the uninvited forgiveness, through God's goodness, of their own immeasurable guilt.[93] Even reflection on the special reward due to those who 'followed' was developed first – as A. Schulz has shown – in the community tradition.[94]

Jesus', SyBU 1 (1943), 26ff.: 'that there can be no question of an eschatological community made possible by the earthly activity of Jesus'. Also: 'Jesus und die Anfänge der Kirche', HuG 289-309 (= StTh 7 (1953), 1-27), and supplementing this critically, E. Grässer, op.cit. (p.15, n.38), 67 n.2. Cf. also H. Conzelmann, RGG 3rd ed., 3.624, 629, 646 (E.T. 21f., 33ff., 79f.): 'It is the fellowship of those who wait'. E. Fuch's definition in *Ges. Aufs.* 2.158 (E.T. 24) – 'an unorganized group of the eschatological community' – already seems to go too far. On Jesus' commissioning of the 'twelve', see E. Meyer, UAC 1.291ff, 296, 299; cf. N. A. Dahl, op.cit. (p.40 n.9), 158; W. G. Kümmel, 'Kirchenbegriff' 30f.; HuG 56, 291f; G. Bornkamm, *JvN*, 138 (E.T. 150); E. Schweizer, *Gemeinde und Gemeindeordnung im NT*, AThANT 35 (1959), 22. On the demand to all Israel, see 1 Kings 18.31: Elijah's altar made of 12 stones; 11.30: the mantle of the prophet Ahijah cut up into 12 pieces before Jeroboam; cf. also Judg 19.29 and 1 Sam 11.7.

[92] Against E. Percy, op.cit. (p.1 n.2), 168-174. Cf. on the other hand H. Conzelmann, RGG 3rd ed., 3.629 (E.T. 35): 'Time and again he calls people into discipleship and this discipleship is demanded unconditionally. But Jesus does not make this discipleship in the external sense a general condition for salvation, i.e. he establishes no sect'; G. Bornkamm, JvN, 136 (E.T. 147), who distinguishes 'the disciples as a more intimate group from Jesus' followers in the wider sense' and is followed by H. E. Tödt, *Menschensohn*, 280 (E.T. 309f.); cf. also W. G. Kümmel, HuG 291; A. Schulz, op.cit. (p.1 n.1), 95ff.; E. Haenchen, *Weg Jesu*, 108 n.5.

[93] On Jesus' preaching of God's eschatological will, see R. Bultmann, *Jesus*, 69-122 (E.T. 58-97); *Theologie des NT* 11ff., 17ff. (E.T. 11ff., 18ff.). On the demand for conversion and obedience see H. Braun, *Radikalismus* 2.29-61, especially in relation to the rigorist Essene movement. Cf. also G. Bornkamm, JvN, 74ff., 92-118 (E.T. 82ff., 100-129) and C. H. Dodd, l. c. (n.31): Jesus appears 'in the Gospels rather as a preacher of repentance than as a teacher in the usual sense. His μετανοεῖτε is an echo of the prophetic שׁוּב.'

[94] Op.cit. (p.1 n.1), 117-125.

The objection that we are importing into Jesus' proclamation the alien idea of 'double discipleship' can hardly be sustained for it was not the aim of the historical Jesus' preaching that all his hearers should be his 'disciples' in the proper sense of the word. It was not he himself and his person and authority which constituted the core of his proclamation but the absoluteness of the divine will in regard to the proximity of the breaking in of the βασιλεία τοῦ θεοῦ. If Jesus nevertheless spoke about his commission and authority, he did so not as an end in itself but in order to designate his call to decision as the ultimate and definitive call.[95] His hearers were to decide primarily not for Jesus' person but for his message of the nearness of the gracious and judging God, although seen as a whole Jesus' proclamation cannot be divorced from his person, the more so since it was supplemented by his healings, in which it becomes clear symbolically 'that the Kingdom of God... is at hand'.[96] Only once the 'proclaimer' had become the 'proclaimed' were 'following after' and 'faith' identified, the 'disciples' becoming the believing community. But even here it is still noticeable that the term 'following after' (ἀκολουθεῖν) in connection with Jesus appears outside the Gospels only once and then in the figurative sense (Rev 14.4: οὗτοι οἱ ἀκολουθοῦντες τῷ ἀρνίῳ ὅπου ἂν ὑπάγῃ), just as in very similar fashion the expression μαθητής appears solely in Acts, again in the sense of 'believers'.[97] On the other hand, somewhat surprisingly, the Pauline idea of μίμησις Χριστοῦ (cf. I Cor 11.1) relates primarily to the sufferings of Christ and not to the concrete 'following' by Jesus' disciples although it is possible to establish an overarching connection between the two, in the sense that they both refer to the believers' unconditional sharing of a common destiny with Christ. Closest to Paul's idea is the saying about carrying one's cross, which occurs in differing forms in the Mark and Q traditions.[98] If one really takes the view – with e.g. E. Percy – that Jesus called the *entire people* without distinction to 'follow after' him, this would be to bring him dangerously close to those apocalyptic enthusiasts who called the Jewish population of Palestine to 'follow' them as if they were a second Moses, for an interpretation of ἀκολουθεῖν or ἔρχεσθαι ὀπίσω which simply assumes that it is to be taken in the figurative sense of 'believing' or

[95] R. Bultmann, *Theologie d. NT*, 8 (E.T. 9): 'Basically... he is in his own person the "sign of the time".' Cf. e.g. Mt 11.3-6 = Lk 7.19-23; Mt 12.41f. = Lk 11.31; Mt 12.28 = Lk 11.20. There are also some individual ἦλθον sayings like Mk 2.17//s cf. Lk 19.10; Mt 10.34, cf. Lk 12.49; Mt 11.18f. = Lk 7.33 which may belong in this context. See now on this J. Jeremias, ZNW 58 (1967), 167.

[96] R. Bultmann, op.cit. 6, cf. E. Grässer, op.cit. 6 n.3.

[97] See A. Schulz, op.cit. 137-179. But cf. 1 Pet 2.21.

[98] On Paul as μιμητὴς τοῦ Χριστοῦ 1 Cor 11.1 cf. P. Stuhlmacher, EvTh 27 (1967), 32. Closest to the saying about 'carrying one's cross' are the Pauline sayings on suffering with Christ (συμπάσχειν Rom 8.17; συσταυροῦσθαι Gal 2.19, cf. Rom 6.6). See also 2 Cor 1.5; 4.10; Gal 6.14; Phil 3.10. The completely one-sided derivation of the Pauline *mimēsis Christi* from the idea of *mimēsis* in the mystery religions, in H. D. Betz op.cit. (p.1 n.2), 137ff. is not at all convincing. See also below, pp.84ff.

'obeying' is completely unjustified. Rather must we differentiate clearly between the later interpretation of 'following after' in the Gospels and the original sense of Jesus' call to follow him.

6 Prophetic and charismatic features in the activity of Jesus

We could of course, against the thesis of the dominant preponderance of the 'charismatic and prophetic' element in Jesus' activity, enter the consideration that in the Synoptics it is only seldom that those elements are discernible which are commonly related to the prophetic consciousness. Neither can we demonstrate the existence of an experience of a prophetic call in Jesus,[99] nor can we find unambiguously clear pointers to visions, ecstatic experiences and the like. Nor does he anywhere present his message with the introductory formulae which are typical of the O.T. prophets and arose out of heralds' proclamations – such as 'Thus saith the Lord' or 'The saying of the Lord' or the like – formulae which were picked up again by early Christian prophets, who transferred them to the Spirit.[100] Nor does the 'Spirit of God' play any decisive part in the Synoptics in relation to Jesus' activities, and when it does appear, the traditions are mostly secondary – most strikingly so in Lk 4.1, 14, 18f. (Is 61.1ff.); but even 'Luke avoids the idea that the Spirit is superior to Jesus'.[101] In themselves these observations are to a great extent acceptable, but it must be asked how far in New Testament times a visionary experience of a call and fixed introductory formulae were still constitutive of the 'prophetic' preacher; even as regards John the Baptist nothing of the kind is reported; it is not until Lk 3.1 that his appearance is presented in a way which clearly depends on Jer 1.1(LXX). On the other hand, where the problem of the small significance which attaches to the Spirit in the case of Jesus is concerned, we should have to consider whether the reason for its rare appearances in the original tradition is that Jesus did not need to have to resort to the Spirit as an intermediary, given his unique claim to authority, drawn as it was from the immediacy of his relation to God. Thus, the reason why the Spirit had to give place was not because Jesus taught with the rational certainty of a *demonstration* based on exegesis or 'wisdom'; on the contrary it was because he appeared with

[99] H. Windisch's assumptions, op.cit. (p.25 n.31), 120ff., 135f. are rather unconvincing. Perhaps the story of the baptism can be turned into a 'call vision'.

[100] See R. Rendtorff, ThW 6.801, 810f (E.T. 6.800, 809f.). On the NT prophets see E. Schweizer, op.cit. (p.1 n.2), 39 n.163, drawing attention to Acts 2.1ff. and Mt 7.22. Cf also Acts 11.28; 21.11; Rev 14.13b; Lk 11.49 could also have been uttered by such prophets.

[101] E. Schweizer, ThW 7.398ff. (cit. 402.13f.) (E.T. 6.396ff.). Cf. also H. Windisch in *Studies in Early Christianity,* ed. S. J. Case 1928, 209-236. In detail, C. K. Barrett, *The Holy Spirit and the Gospel Tradition,* 1947, *passim,* see above all ch.10: Why do the Gospels say so little about the Spirit? 140-162, where Barrett among other things points to the fact that even the OT prophets relatively seldom claim for themselves the designation *nābî'* or claim the Spirit as their authority, 148f.

a *'charismatic authority'* which wholly transcended that of contemporary apocalyptic prophets.[102] We shall have to come back to this decisive point for understanding Jesus.

On the other hand the Synoptic Gospels do retain some hints that can not be overlooked, and are such as could have been conditioned by visionary aptitude on the part of Jesus. We shall cautiously have to exclude the report of Jesus' baptism, the Temptation story, and the accounts of his walking on the water, as these cannot with full assurance be traced back to events óf this kind. However, attempts to account for some of them as resurrection appearances remain just as questionable; but they do show that the community tradition ascribed to Jesus a series of visionary experiences or 'epiphanies'.[103] What may perhaps take us farther is the note in Mk 3.21, which certainly goes back to the historical Jesus, but was eliminated by Mt and Lk because it was offensive, and which proves that Jesus' behaviour, breaking as it did the bounds of all the conventions, had among his closest relatives given cause for offence and annoyance to the extent that they reproached him with being mad or possessed: καὶ ἀκούσαντες οἱ παρ' αὐτοῦ ἐξῆλθον κρατῆσαι αὐτόν· ἔλεγον γὰρ ὅτι ἐξέστη. This episode is supplemented and illuminated by the brusque rejection of Jesus in Nazareth, Mk 6.1-6:v.3f. . . . καὶ ἐσκανδαλίζοντο ἐν αὐτῷ. καὶ ἔλεγεν αὐτοῖς ὁ Ἰησοῦς ὅτι οὐκ ἔστιν προφήτης ἄτιμος εἰ μὴ ἐν τῇ πατρίδι αὐτοῦ καὶ ἐν τοῖς συγγενεῦσιν αὐτοῦ καὶ ἐν τῇ οἰκίᾳ αὐτοῦ. Both scenes remind one of Jeremiah's relations with relatives in Anathoth.[104] Here too Matthew and Luke have

[102] This seems more probable to me than does C. K. Barrett's thesis, op.cit. 158: 'Direct emphasis upon the Spirit had to be avoided also because Jesus was keeping his Messiahship secret; to have claimed a pre-eminent measure of the Spirit would have been to make an open confession of Messiahship'; also 119f. Nor is one convinced by H. Windisch's thesis, op.cit. (n.101), 231ff., that the early Synoptic tradition suppressed the events of the Spirit's activity. Later, indeed, the tradition re-emphasized them. One will necessarily have to distinguish between the undoubted prophetic and charismatic activity of Jesus and the lack of references to the 'Spirit'. It is quite likely that, by contrast with Jesus, contemporary apocalyptic-messianic prophets appealed freely to the 'Spirit'. According to the Essene texts and apocalyptic literature there was in Judaism nothing unusual in appealing to actual possession of the Spirit between the Maccabean period and 70 AD, the more so as expectation of the nearness of the Eschaton was relatively widespread among the people (see M. Hengel, *Zeloten*, 316). According to T Pes 4.2 (1.163) even Hillel gave all Israel the benefit of having possession of the Spirit: 'Leave them, the Holy Spirit is upon them; if they are not prophets, they are the sons of the prophets'; cf. on this E. Sjöberg, ThW 6.384 (E.T. 6.382ff.). Presumably later rabbinic tradition suppressed these views as a result of its greater institutionalization.

[103] On the subject of Jesus' possible 'ecstatic experiences', see C. H. Dodd, (p.46 n.31), 76: see G. Friedrich, ThW 6.844, 18ff., who rightly rules out a number of possible references to such occurrences. O. Holtzmann in *War Jesus Ekstatiker?*, 1908 and H. Windisch in *Paulus u. Christus*, 179ff. go much too far.

[104] Jer 12.6: 'Even your brethren, your father's house, deal treacherously with you, they too are in full cry after you'; 11.21: the 'men of Anathoth' threaten the prophet, 'Do not prophesy in the name of the Lord, or you will die by our hand'. Cf. also 9.3.

again made corresponding emendations (Mt 13.53ff.; Lk 4.16ff.). Had Jesus been a rabbi learned in the Torah or a teacher of wisdom like Ben Sira he would doubtless have met with a more positive reception, and with someone of that sort the closest members of his family would hardly have set out to fetch him back home.[105] Perhaps H. Windisch was too bold in contrasting that ὅτι ἐξέστη with what Paul says in II Cor 5.13: εἴτε γὰρ ἐξέστημεν, θεῷ· εἴτε σωφρονοῦμεν, ὑμῖν. 'The pneumatic lives in two spheres: in ecstasy which leads him up to God, and in the sphere of the self-possessed νοῦς.'[106] Even if we cannot share the far-reaching conclusions on Jesus as an 'ecstatic' which Windisch in fact draws from the scene in Mk 3.20f, we must nevertheless admit that here we are told of a feature in Jesus' activity which on the whole falls into the background in the Synoptic Gospels because it runs counter to the trend in their tradition. Even R. Bultmann asks 'whether the tradition has not suppressed the prophetic apocalyptic character of Jesus' appearance in favour of his teaching activity as a rabbi'.[107] It appears most strongly in the tradition, which to us is extremely alien, of Jesus as an exorcist, i.e. in the context of his struggle with the powers of evil. This above all in the cry of victory in Lk 10.18: ἐθεώρουν τὸν σατανᾶν ὡς ἀστραπὴν ἐκ τοῦ οὐρανοῦ πεσόντα. This saying of Jesus, which I take to be genuine – for what primitive Christian prophet would have had the authority to make such a pronouncement, ἐθεώρουν?[108] – is closely linked with the other authoritative saying likewise going back to Jesus: εἰ δὲ ἐν δακτύλῳ θεοῦ ἐγὼ (𝔓75 א1 BCLR al D) ἐκβάλλω τὰ δαιμόνια, ἄρα ἔφθασεν ἐφ᾽ ὑμᾶς ἡ βασιλεία τοῦ θεοῦ.[109] In his exorcisms Jesus participates in the power of God; they are 'an expression of the direct and concrete intervention of God', comparable with the wonders at the creation, at the Exodus from Egypt, and the coming into existence of the tables of the Law, written on by God's finger.[110] He is the ἰσχυρότερος, who conquers the ἰσχυρός and

[105] See above pp.31f.: the change of mind by the father of Eliezer b. Hyrcanus and of Akiba's father-in-law.

[106] Op.cit., 180. Cf. also C. K. Barrett, op.cit. (n.101), 96 on Mk 3.21, 30: ἐξέστη ... πνεῦμα ἀκάθαρτον (see above, pp.40ff.): 'These both attest a sort of prophetic frenzy, a spirit-possession the immediate outward results of which would vary little if the spirit were a demon or the Holy Spirit', cf. Hos 9.7.

[107] Synoptische Tradition 52, cf. 113 (E.T. 50, cf. 108f.). In detail, C. K. Barrett, op.cit. 68, 90-93, 98f., 144 on n.1. See also G. Friedrich, ThW 6.845, 26ff. (E.T. 6.843).

[108] Cf. G. Friedrich, loc. cit., n.395 (E.T. 6.843 n.395). According to R. Bultmann op.cit. 113 (E.T. 108) this is the sole saying to merit consideration as the 'report of a vision': 'it gives a strong impression of being a fragment' (174).

[109] Lk 11.20 (cf. Mt 12.28: εἰ δὲ ἐν πνεύματι θεοῦ ...), on which see R. G. Hamerton Kelly, NTS 11 (1964/65), 167-169, though his thesis of the originality of Mt's version does not admittedly carry conviction. Lk, who introduces a strengthened form of the 'pneuma' concept into his Gospel, would assuredly not have turned πνεύματι in the text before him into the anthromorphic δακτύλῳ. On the question of the future and present aspects of the Kingdom of God, in relation to this passage, see H. W. Kuhn, Enderwartung und gegenwärtiges Heil, SUNT 4 (1965), 190-193. Here we have to remember that this was formulated as polemics.   [110] H. Schlier, ThW 2.21.9ff. (E.T. 2.21); Bill 2.187.

deprives him of his booty (Lk 11.21-23 Q, cf. Mk 3.27 = Mt 12.29). Such pronouncements go beyond even the consciousness of his mission which characterized contemporary apocalyptic-messianic prophets of the *Moses redivivus* type. The victory which occurs in Jesus' healings, over the power of Satan, which manifests itself in illness and possession, means the signal and visible 'dawn' of the rule of God. A heavenly event corresponds to this victory: the fall of Satan, the Accuser before God.[111] Probably Jesus' activity as an 'exorcist' and 'healer of the sick' awakened among the simple Galilean population at least as much attention and enthusiasm as his preaching. It can be seen that this part of his activity (which we find so hard to understand today) was also given great importance in the early tradition of the community, for in the tradition about the Mission of the disciples the Twelve specifically receive authority to exorcise and to heal the sick and according to the Q tradition they extol their successes after they come back.[112] Even an old *baraita* knows of the Jewish Christians of Palestine having authority 'to heal' those who have fallen seriously ill 'in the name of Jesus (ben Pantera)' (T Hull 2.22f., p.503: לרפאותו משום ישוע בן פנטרא) and of this being gladly made use of by the non-Christian Jewish population despite the objections of individual rabbis.[113]

Jesus' beatitude in Lk 10.23f. = Mt 13.16f. (Q) shows that he himself understood his activity as something that was eschatologically definitive and absolute: μακάριοι οἱ ὀφθαλμοὶ οἱ βλέποντες ἃ βλέπετε to be supplemented thus according to Mt: καὶ τὰ ὦτα (τὰ ἀκούοντα ἃ ἀκούετε).ἀμὴν γὰρ λέγω (Mt) ὑμῖν ὅτι πολλοὶ προφῆται καὶ βασιλεῖς (Lk) ἠθέλησαν ἰδεῖν ἃ ὑμεῖς βλέπετε καὶ οὐκ εἶδαν καὶ ἀκοῦσαι ἃ ἀκούετε καὶ οὐκ ἤκουσαν. His answer to John the Baptist has a very similar drift (Lk 7.22f. = Mt 11.5), as does the figure of the presence of the bridegroom in Mk 2.19a. In his preaching, his miracles of healing and his fellowship with taxgatherers and sinners the rule of God is already presently active in advance as a 'realm of wholeness and salvation (Heilssphäre)', and in a real sense is 'already beginning'.[114] Whether we describe Jesus as a 'rabbi' or as a wisdom teacher and prophet we shall equally fail to do justice to this unheard of self-confidence which cuts across all the analogies in the field of *Religionsgeschichte* which are known to us from contemporary Judaism.

[111] See A. Schlatter, *Das Evangelium des Lc,* 1960, 2nd ed., 279; cf. W. Grundmann, *Das Evangelium n. Lc,* ThHK, 2nd ed., 1964, 212.

[112] Authority to heal the sick and to exorcise: Mk 6.7, 13; Lk 9.1f., 6; 10.9; Mt 10.8. On their return, see Lk 10.17, 19f.

[113] //s AZ 27b; jShab 14b/15a and jAZ 40b/41a; cf. J. Klausner, op.cit. (n.14), 47f. (E.T. 40) and R. and M. Hengel, op.cit. (n.88), 356f. This would have been around 100 AD. On healing 'in the name of Jesus' cf. also Mk 9.38f.; Lk 9.49; 10.17; Acts 4.30, where the usage of the community is everywhere presupposed.

[114] On this, see H. W. Kuhn, op.cit. (n.109), 189-204. On Lk 10.24 = Mt 13.17 see MekEx 15.2 (L 2.24), cf. Bill 1.664; R. Eliezer b. Hyrcanus: a female slave at the Red Sea saw what Isaiah, Ezekiel and all the other prophets did not see.

7 The unique 'messianic' authority of Jesus

We cannot go in detail into the central question of Jesus' *teaching* but would like simply to stress that as a totality it was presented with *charismatic authority* even although in part it had the stamp of 'wisdom' about it. Jesus neither follows the rabbinical method of deducing it from the Torah as prescribed in the schools, nor does he, like the teachers of wisdom of an earlier age, appeal to the evidential force of his teaching, based on observation and experience. The radicalised demand for love of one's neighbour, resulting in renunciation of violence and rejection of loveless ritualism; the pointlessness of worry and the unconditional nature of forgiveness; the condemnation of all self-assurance and self-righteousness: his whole 'ethical' preaching can be seen as an *eschatologically preconditioned* expression of his charismatically based call to decision. The pressing forcefulness of this call is legitimately described by all three evangelists by their use of the term ἐξουσία (Mk 1.22, 27 = Mt 7.29: cf. Lk 4.32, 36. See also Mk 2.10//s and Mk 11.28f.//s), which likewise characterizes Jesus' preaching and activity. H. Conzelmann rightly emphasizes that the 'teaching and conduct, word and deeds, the *proclamation* and anticipatory *realisation* of salvation form a unity'.[115]

It is thus typical that his deeds and attitudes can at decisive points acquire the *character of parables* – comparably with the Old Testament prophets but transcending them.[116] His demonstrative and offensive table-fellowship with taxgatherers and sinners points to the eschatological banquet in the Kingdom of God, where the standards of piety which have thus far held good will be turned completely upside down. Here basically the Pauline idea of *justificatio impii* is anticipated, and it is entirely of a piece with this that Jesus also forgave sins, as with the paralytic.[117] When he puts a child in the midst of the disciples, and embraces and blesses the children against his disciples' will, we see that

[115] H. Conzelmann, RGG 3rd ed., 3.628 (E.T. 7f.), cf. R. Bultmann, *Glauben u. Verstehen*, 1933, 1.274 (E.T. *Faith and Understanding*, 1966, 283), based on the interpretation of Mk 8.38 in Lk 12.8: 'Thus it turns out that Jesus' person is subsumed in his word, which however also means that his word is Event . . . an Event of the power and will of God like the prophetic word in Israel'.

[116] The scope of Jesus' 'parabolic' action is hard to define. G. Stählin, 'Die Gleichnishandlungen Jesu' in *Kosmos u. Ekklesia, Festschrift für W. Stählin*, 1953, 9-22, sees it as extensive, whereas F. Hahn, op.cit. (p.4 n.4), 381 n.2 (E.T. 372 and 399 n.155 (abbreviated)), limits it to the Last Supper and, possibly, the cleansing of the Temple; to which Mk 11.13f., 20f. can also be added as a symbolic action that originally developed out of a parable. Perhaps J. Jeremias' survey in *Gleichnisse Jesu*, 1965, 7th ed. (E.T. *The Parables of Jesus*, 1963, 227f.); gives the most accurate list of the real 'parabolic actions'. The entire complex is of course open in relation to Jesus' 'symbolic' activity announcing the nearness of the dawning of the Kingdom with God's salvation and God's judgment.

[117] Cf. Mk 2.1-10//s, on which see G. Bornkamm, JvN, 74 (E.T. 81): cf. also W. G. Kümmel, HuG 123f.

God turns his attention to the weak, the immature and those of little account, who are not expert in the Law and so do not merit the Kingdom of God by their own activities, but can receive it only in trust as an unmerited gift.[118]

We find an example in complete contrast to Jesus' attitude in the pronouncement of R. Ḥanina b. Harkina (beginning of 2nd Century A.D.): 'Holding converse with children and being where the ᶜammê hā'āres gather together take a man out of the world' (Ab 3.10b). There is a more specific justification offered for this in the *gemara* to it in the Aboth de R. Nathan (Vs.A c.21 p.74 Schechter): both keep a man from studying the Law.

The appointment of the Twelve, the historicity of which has been unjustly challenged, indicates that he has come to call *all* Israel to repentance in the light of the nearness of God's rule, and to proclaim salvation to her (see above p.60 n.91). Likewise the Entry into Jerusalem and above all the Cleansing of the Temple may well be understood eschatologically as parabolic actions: Jesus 'cleanses the sanctuary for the approaching Kingdom of God'.[119]

Here too the impression is confirmed that Jesus' claim to authority can best be described by the category of the 'eschatological charismatic', though of course this category at the same time goes far beyond anything that can be adduced as prophetic prototypes or parallels from the field of the Old Testament and from the New Testament period. It would be possible, in fact, to apply to Jesus' teaching and attitudes a comment made by E. Fuchs in relation to the parable of the Prodigal Son: 'Jesus dares to make God's will effective as if he himself stood in God's stead'.[120]

He shatters the power of the evil one, invites sinners to the messianic banquet, makes the claim that his message of the nearness of salvation and of God's judgment is binding without reserve on all Israel, including the Holy City and The Temple. Comparison in the field of *Religionsgeschichte* does in fact confirm these observations. Thus Morton Smith, in his impressive comparison of the Gospels with Tannaitic parallels, comes to the conclusion 'that Jesus appears in the Gospels in a number of

[118] Mk 9.34-37 = Mt 18.1-8 = Lk 9.46-48; Mk 10.13-16 = Mt 19.13-15 = Lk 18.15-17. Here it is also significant that Lk and Mt leave out the wholly unconventional feature of the ἐναγκαλισάμενος of Mk 9.36 and 10.16. Jesus' actions are hardly to be understood in M. Black's terms, op.cit. (p.7 n.15), 264-268, explaining the problem on the basis of the ambiguity of 'ṭalyā' as 'child' and partially also 'young slave'. On the lack of understanding in rabbinic Judaism for children see W. Oepke, ThW 5.644f. (E.T. 5.645ff.), cf. also BN 7.6 and Ter 1.1: minors are compared with the 'deaf' and the 'inane'; they lack 'understanding' (דעת), cf. also the list in Ber 3.3; 7.2: 'women, slaves and children', and also Lk 10.21ff. = Mt 11.25ff. and Mt 21.15f – J. Jeremias, op.cit. (n.40) following T. W. Manson, draws attention to the fact that the rabbis were not familiar with the linking of children with humility. But Jesus' attitude is completely unrabbinic anyway.

[119] G. Bornkamm, JvN, 146 (E.T. 159).

[120] *Ges. Aufsätze* 2.154, 156 (E.T. 22): 'This conduct' (of Jesus) 'is, neither that of a prophet nor that of a teacher of wisdom, but that of a man who dares to act in God's stead'.

places where the parallel passages of T(annaitic) L(iterature) have God or the Law'.[121]

In accordance with this unique claim we have 'abbā as the form for addressing God in prayer, a form unusual in older Palestinian Judaism,[122] or again the reinforcement of what Jesus says by the introductory formula ἀμὴν λέγω ὑμῖν which is likewise novel.[123] T. W. Manson, followed by J. Jeremias, was probably right in supposing that it was Jesus' desire to use this to replace the authoritative prophetic formula, 'Thus saith the Lord'.[124] As Jesus here substitutes his 'I say unto you' for an address by God, he will have not merely replaced the prophetic formula, but consciously have sought to surpass it. It would be possible to speak in this connection of the 'immediacy of his relation to God', his 'certainty of God', and those loath to use such 'psychologising' terms may speak of his unique, underivable claim to authority, grounded in God himself.[125] Quite certainly Jesus was not a 'teacher' comparable with the later rabbinical experts in the Law, and he was a great deal more than a prophet. Even within the characterization we have preferred, of an 'eschatological charismatic', he remains in the last resort incommensurable, and so basically confounds every attempt to fit him into the categories suggested by the phenomenology or sociology of religion.[126] Consequently, the centrality, in recent discussion, of the phenomenon of the underivable nature of *Jesus' authority,* is fully justified. One can find no better adjective than 'messianic' to describe it.[127]

[121] M. Smith, *Tannaitic Parallels to the Gospels,* JBL Monograph Ser. 6 (1951), 159.

[122] J. Jeremias, *Abba,* 1964, 1-67, esp. 57ff.: cf. 145ff. (E.T. 11-65, esp. 66ff.).

[123] Op.cit. 148ff.; E. Käsemann agrees, EVuB 1.209 (E.T. 40ff.): 'it signifies an extreme and immediate certainty such as is conveyed by inspiration' (E.T. 42).

[124] T. W. Manson, *The Teaching of Jesus,* 2nd ed., reprint of 1948, 207, with J. Jeremias agreeing, op.cit. 149 n.21. Cf. the reflections of A. Schlatter, *Mt,* 155.

[125] Cf. G. Bornkamm, JvN, 52 (E.T. 57): 'There is nothing in contemporary Judaism which corresponds to the immediacy with which he teaches . . .' On the term 'Gottesgewissheit' (certainty of God), see E. Fuchs, *Ges. Aufs.* II. 364f., 397f. and G. Ebeling, *Theologie und Verkündigung,* 1963 2nd ed., 91; cf. also 119ff. (E.T. *Theology and Proclamation,* 90, cf. 124ff.). See further E. Käsemann, EVuB 1.210 (E.T. 42): 'It is by this immediate assurance of knowing and proclaiming the will of God that Jesus is distinguished from the rabbis'. 2.109 (E.T. 112): 'Liberalism, too, saw a point of cardinal importance when it emphasized the immediacy of the relation of Jesus to God as Father'.

[126] See G. van der Leeuw, *Phänomenologie d. Religion,* 1956 2nd ed., 765f. (E.T. 666f.): 'For Christian faith the figure of the mediator is no "phenomenon"; the phenomenologist cannot perceive where and how it enters history. He observes *prophet,* reformer, *teacher,* example; but he cannot show the *mediator in his historical effectiveness*... he can perceive that Jesus sacrificed himself; but he can only believe that Jesus was none other than God giving himself' (my italics). Cf. also E. Käsemann, EVuB 2.117f. (E.T. 121ff.) on the 'uniqueness of him who is bringing salvation' and the category of the 'mediator who brings in the eschatological age by the act of announcing it' (E.T. 122). By comparison, despite some interesting detailed comments, the portrayal of Jesus as a 'primitive charismatic' in R. Otto, op.cit. (n.61), 277-309 (E.T. 333-345ff.), does not recognise the limits of the method of the phenomenology of religion, and this is where its weakness lies.

[127] O. Michel, EvTh 15 (1955), 355: 'The collection of individual sayings, anecdotes and

Jesus' claim to authority gains its ultimate sharpness from the simply *sovereign attitude* he adopts *towards the Law of Moses*. This is where we find the fundamental point of distinction over against Pharisaism and the charismatic, apocalyptic trends within Judaism, including Essenism and the Baptist movements. For him the Mosaic Torah no longer constituted the focal point and the ultimately valid standard. Jesus did not stand under the authority of the Torah received at Sinai by Moses – as all his Jewish contemporaries did – but stood above it.[128] His sayings, 'Behold, a greater than Solomon is here' and 'Behold, a greater than Jonah is here' (Lk 11.31f. = Mt 12.41f.Q), could be supplemented in the light of this by 'Behold, something greater than Moses is here'. This is proved by the antitheses of the Sermon on the Mount, even if their formulation as such should come from the community tradition.[129] Deeply conscious of the inbreaking of God's rule, Jesus for the first time in Judaism looks behind the Law of Moses towards the original will of God:

> 'The discussion is about what the ultimate criterion is to be: direct receipt of instructions to the elect, or Moses' commandment with its frequent allowances for human weakness. The *Messianic* element is the *rediscovery of what was original·and of what is in accordance with the Creation,* of the unbroken and radical knowledge of God.'[130]

As the authority of the Law as a whole was involved in any criticism of a part of it, given the 'ontological' understanding of the Torah[131] predominating with its cosmological anchoring in the New Testament period, the later development of the Hellenistic Jewish community is in its core already foreshadowed in the message of Jesus, which therefore can no longer be given a place within contemporary Judaism (as R.

---

miracles of Jesus has as their presupposition the surprise prompted by the *authority of Jesus*' (author's italics), (Mt 7.28-29), and this surprise or terror at Jesus' authority is one of the most important elements in the formation of the Gospels'. See also R. Bultmann, SAH 1960, H.3.11, 17; G. Bornkamm, JvN, 52 (E.T. 57), E. Fuchs, *Ges. Aufs.* II. 256; *Glaube u. Erfahrung, Ges. Aufs.* III. 1965, 11f., 22; E. Schweizer, *Neotestamentica,* 1963, 146; P. Vielhauer, *Aufs z. NT,* 90; G. Ebeling, op.cit. (n.125), 75, 96 (E.T. 98): 'The very diverse expressions of his authority: his teaching, casting out demons, forgiveness of sins, his freedom from legalism, and his call to discipleship' (my italics) 'have at least this in common, that by setting men free they assert the nearness of God as the ἐξουσία of the Word . . . .' On the concept of the 'Messianic' see E. Käsemann, EVuB 1.206 (E.T. 37f.): 'The only category which does justice to his claim (quite independently of whether he used it himself and required it of others) is . . . that of the "Messiah".'

[128] To similar effect already, E. v. Dobschütz, 'The attitude of Jesus and St Paul toward the Bible', The Bible Magazine, 1910 (not accessible to me), as in O. Michel, op.cit. (n.35), 187f.

[129] On the 'antitheses' see P. Stuhlmacher, *Gerechtigkeit Gottes,* FRLANT 87 (1965), 249-252: 'the substance of the "antitheses" draws our attention forcibly to the person of the speaker': cf. also H. F. Weiss, op.cit. (n.47), 117 n.1.

[130] O. Michel, op.cit. (n.3), 314.

[131] On Torah ontology see M. Hengel, op.cit. (p.27 n.41), 311ff (E.T. 171ff.).

Bultmann attempted) without basically shattering the framework of Judaism.[132]

Likewise that provocative and unsurpassable sharpness in Jesus' answer to the prospective disciple of Mt 8.21f., which was our starting-point, can be understood only in this overall context. It is rooted in the sovereign claim to messianic authority which also lies behind Jesus' call to follow him.

The question whether and how far this 'claim to messianic authority' implies the assumption by Jesus of 'messianic honorific titles', we cannot deal with in this setting. However it seems very questionable to me whether we can go on adhering as a matter of principle to the thesis, so popular at present, of a Jesus wholly devoid of titles, given the unique 'authority' of Jesus which has its acme in the fact that he 'dares to act in God's stead'.[133] Certainly, this is one way of disentangling Jesus from the *Religionsgeschichte* of Judaism, but it is a procedure which, while facilitating our modern understanding of Jesus, can hardly be justified in relation to the historical Jesus in 30 A.D. At the least, the enigmatic designation 'Son of Man' is too firmly anchored in Jesus' own pronouncements about himself.[134]

8 The meaning of Jesus' call to follow him

Jesus' call to follow him can now also be seen in its correct light. Just as in the Old Testament God himself called individual prophets from work and family – 'and Yahweh took me from the flock and said to me "Go and prophesy against my people Israel" ' (Amos 7.15) – so Jesus also calls individuals away from all human ties to follow him. Thus there are indeed good grounds for the stylization of the Synoptic discipleship pericopae in terms of the call of Elisha by Elijah or of the prophetic vocation generally

[132] See *Theologie des NT,* 1ff. (E.T. 1ff.); *Das Urchristentum,* rde 157/8, 1962, 67ff. (E.T. *Primitive Christianity in its contemporary setting,* 1956, 69ff.). With qualifications, SAH 1960 H. 3.8f. Contrariwise, E. Käsemann, EVuB 2.47f., 60 (E.T. 40ff., 55f.): 'The Torah is indivisible.... But Jesus refused to accept this indivisibility. For me this is where his transcendence of Judaism is most clearly revealed'; cf. W. Eltester, ZNW 43 (1950/51), 275ff.

[133] E. Fuchs, *Ges. Aufs.* II. 156; (E.T. 22), similarly J. Jeremias, op.cit. (n.116), 132, and E. Jüngel, op.cit. (n.40), 133.

[134] On this, W. G. Kümmel, HuG 404f., cf. also ThR 31 (1966), 304 in discussion with G. Bornkamm, *JvN.* See also E. Schweizer, op.cit. (p.1 n.2), 33-52 (E.T. 32-55). R. E. C. Formesyn's supposition in NovTest 8 (1966), 1-35, since re-stated, has much to be said for it: viz. that with the original *bar enaš* we may have to do with a circumlocution for the first person singular pronoun, i.e. 'I'. Cf. e.g. jShab 3a/b, where R. Simeon b. Joḥai paraphrases a reference to himself, in a context which is given special emphasis, viz. what in Moses' place on Mt Sinai he would have asked for himself, using להדין בר נשא: 'that this man (=I) should have been given two mouths, one for the Law, and one for all other purposes'. This linguistic usage appears here as a conscious circumlocution or paraphrase; cf. also 2 Cor 12.2, 3.

(see p.16ff. above). Here 'following' means in the first place unconditional *sharing of the master's destiny*, which does not stop even at
deprivation and suffering in the train of the master, and is possible only
on the basis of complete trust on the part of the person who 'follows'; he
has placed his destiny and his future in his master's hands.

However, this question at once presents itself to us: for what *purpose*
did Jesus call quite specific individuals to follow him in this absolutely
binding way? Why did he tie them thus to his way and to his destiny?
What is it that adequately justifies this demand for the abandonment of all
human ties and obligations, and even indeed the break with Law and
custom? The total 'freedom' of the individual certainly did not have for
him that absolute intrinsic value which it had for the Cynics and Stoics. In
other words, what, concretely, was the will of God for those 'followers'
whom Jesus called to share their lives with him, under the impact of the
dawning of the Basileia? His popular preaching of the nearness of the
Kingdom, and his healings, would have been conceivable even without
the actual calling of disciples, and in the oldest traditional material he
often appears as the one who acts alone, without always being surround-
ed by disciples. Conzelmann is right in saying 'The twelve function largely
as "extras" '[135] but this for all practical purposes means that in the
Gospels they fall wholly into the background behind the person of Jesus
(see below p.79f.). On the other hand it is all the more true that they
cannot just be eliminated from the story of Jesus. Neither the rise of the
early Church nor the formation of the Gospel tradition about Jesus would
be conceivable without them. But since neither the rabbinical teacher-
pupil relationship nor – despite some siginificant analogies – the 'following' of charismatic, eschatological prophets by the people yields an
adequate explanation for Jesus' 'call to discipleship', we must look else-
where for its origins.

Following Jesus did not constitute – as it did with the apocalyptic
prophets promising the second Exodus into the desert, with its miracles –
the absolute presupposition for participation in the rule of God, and
therefore it could not be an end in itself. The disciples were not privileged
people who were to be initiated into the esoteric wisdom of the master;
nor did they constitute the exclusive community of those who alone were
the 'elect' of the Kingdom of God. Likewise it was not their task to 'learn'
their master's exposition of the Torah and the exemplary *halakah* of his
way of living, or to 'serve' him in the rabbinic manner (see above,
p.50ff.). Even less did Jesus need any royal, 'messianic' household such
as we find with some Zealot leaders or in the instance of the physician
Menecrates Zeus;[136] nor, finally, could any specially valuable celestial
reward – of somewhat more than average size – provide an adequate

---

[135] Conzelmann, RGG 3rd ed., 3.629 (E.T. 34f.).
[136] Cf. e.g. the shepherd Athronges and his four brothers, *Bell* 2.60f. – *Ant* 17.279ff. or
Menaham, *Bell* 2.434, 444.

motive and goal for following him. Yet we should not abandon the idea that it was thought of as a *meaningful task*. Now if – and this seems the most probable account – Jesus really did express an absolute demand in his call to 'follow' him similar to what is discernible in *the calls of the Old Testament prophets by God*, the solution to the problem might be looked for here:

Moses was called and sent 'to lead God's people out of Egypt' (Ex 3.11), and Gideon to 'save Israel from the hands of the Midianites' (Judg 6.14), Amos 'to prophesy against my people' (Amos 7.15) and Jeremiah to be 'a prophet for the nations, to overthrow and to destroy, to plant and to build up' (1.5, 10). This list could be continued, and its sense is clear: Jahweh called his 'prophets' to proclaim judgment and salvation to his people, and indeed to execute it directly on them (cf. 1 Kings 19.15-18).

May we not suppose that Jesus called his disciples in an analogous way to participate in his mission and authority, in the eschatological event which taking its beginning in him was moving powerfully towards the complete dawn of the rule of God $\dot{\epsilon}\nu$ $\delta\upsilon\nu\acute{\alpha}\mu\epsilon\iota$ (Mk 9.1, cf.13.26//s); that he called them to participate by confronting the whole people, along with him, with the offer of approaching salvation and with the proclamation of the final judgment? But this would mean that *following Jesus* would be comprehensible only as *service to the cause of the approaching Kingdom of God*.[137] Thus the explanatory supplement in Lk 9.60b to the saying of Jesus which was our starting-point – $\sigma\grave{\upsilon}$ $\delta\grave{\epsilon}$ $\dot{\alpha}\pi\epsilon\lambda\theta\grave{\omega}\nu$ $\delta\iota\acute{\alpha}\gamma\gamma\epsilon\lambda\epsilon$ $\tau\grave{\eta}\nu$ $\beta\alpha\sigma\iota\lambda\epsilon\acute{\iota}\alpha\nu$ $\tau o\widehat{\upsilon}$ $\theta\epsilon o\widehat{\upsilon}$ would certainly not be without foundation in substance.

9 The tradition of the sending out of the disciples

Both Mark and the Q tradition agree that – at a time which of course we do not know and can no longer establish – *Jesus sent out his disciples*, and that they proclaimed the message of repentance or of the immediate proximity of the rule of God. Inseparably linked with this was authority over the demons and the commission to heal the sick.[138] To be sure the

---

[137] See H. D. Wendland, *Die Eschatologie des Reiches Gottes bei Jesus*, 1931, 153: 'Accordingly it cannot . . . simply be a question of an analogy with the groups of disciples which the rabbis used to gather round themselves. Rather does the coming rule of God determine the extent to which *this* 'teacher' is supported and the extent of service and 'following' in *this* matter. The unconditional nature of the will of God encountered by such men in the rule of God puts the stamp of total obedience and service on their discipleship' (author's italics). Cf. also e.g. E. Käsemann, EVuB 2.228 (E.T. 39): 'The mission precedes faith and alone justifies it'.

[138] Preaching of repentance: Mk 6.12; message of the nearness of the Kingdom: Mt 10.7; Lk 9.2; 10.9, 11b. Healings and exorcisms: Mk 6.7, 13//s; Lk 10.2, 9; Mt 10.8 (Q); cf. Lk 10.17 and Mk 9.38. On the analysis, see F. Hahn, *Das Verständnis der Mission im NT*, WMANT 13 (1963), 33-36. Cf. J. Roloff, *Apostolat . . .*, 1965, 150ff.

community tradition has fused almost indissolubly on this point with the inherited older traditions, on the basis of its own multi-layered and rich mission experience, but it would be wrong to replace the over-estimation of the reliability of the tradition of the Mission by A. Schweitzer and the proponents of realised eschatology with an equally unjustified total scepticism.[139] That Jesus did send forth the disciples can hardly be doubted in principle, even if it is no longer possible to reconstruct the circumstances in detail. Anyone who considers the tradition of a Mission to be unhistorical in principle must adequately explain why it was that Jesus called individuals to follow him in such an incomparably rigorous way although he did not wish to found either a royal 'messianic' household or the esoteric nucleus of a community. Taking issue with W. Schmithal's and G. Klein's critical views K. Beyschlag has recently and rightly drawn attention to the point that it is likely that 'the basic data of the Synoptic Mission discourse are already presupposed' in I Cor 9.[139a]

The privilege of accompanying Jesus on his wanderings did not in itself justify the rigorous demands of the master that those who followed him should be absolutely free of all earthly and human ties – indeed, Jesus' entourage also included people on whom he did not impose such an obligation, such as sick people who had been cured[140] or the women from Galilee. And even the fact that the women belonged to the wider circle around Jesus is completely incompatible with understanding him as a teacher like the rabbis, but is logically in line with Jesus' turning towards the weak and the despised: the sinners, the sick and the children.[141]

The rigour of Jesus' demand to those 'followers' who were personally called by him is on the contrary to be explained solely on the basis of their designation for the service of the Basileia – a service to occur only in the

[139] See A. Schweitzer, op.cit. (n.1), 403-417 (E.T. 354ff.). On the historicity of the mission, see F. Hahn, loc. cit., and, especially on the disciples' being sent in pairs, which comes out clearly in the lists of apostles in Mk 3.16-19//s and Rev 1.13, see J. Jeremias, op.cit. (n.122), 135f. Cf. also W. G. Kümmel, HuG, 293 and G. Bornkamm, JvN, 137 (E.T. 149): 'they are most actively drawn into the service of his message and the proclamation of the kingdom's victory'.

[139a] Clemens Romanus... BHTh 35 (1966), 34 ad loc.: cf. especially 1 Cor 9.14.

[140] Cf. e.g. Mk 5.18//s; 10.52//s or Lk 8.2b; cf. 17.14. Even if a miracle-story *topos* is involved here – cf. H. Windisch, op.cit. (p.25 n.31), 68f. and above p.26 n.37 on Menecrates and n.38 on Apollonius – such circumstances suggest themselves.

[141] On the women, see M. Hengel, 'Maria Magdalena und die Frauen als Zeugen', in: *Abraham unser Vater*, Festschrift O. Michel, AGSU 5 (1963), 243ff. On the devaluation of women especially in rabbinic Judaism, see J. Leipoldt, *Die Frau in der antiken Welt und im Urchristentum*, 1962, 49-72, and on the position of women in the synoptic Gospels 81-98. Possibly the attitude in an earlier period was not so downright as it afterwards became; the books of Esther – including the later additions preserved only in Greek – and Judith, which may have come into being around the Maccabean period, might point in this direction, and also the reports of the martyred women of that period in 1 Macc 1.60f., 2 Macc 6.10, 7.41 and also the preservation of the *Song of Solomon,* which was probably finally edited in the third century BC. This may be valid even for diaspora Judaism, as otherwise Jewish missionary activity would hardly have had such successes with pagan women.

manner indicated by Jesus' own activity, i.e. in the proclamation of the
nearness of the Kingdom of God and in deeds of healing. The disciples
are permitted to share directly in Jesus' work: '... (they) are not only his
messengers, they are his *fellow-workers*'.[142]

The saying of Jesus placed by the Q Tradition at the beginning of its
account of the Mission (Mt 9.37f. – Lk 10.2 agreeing *verbatim*) – ὁ μὲν
θερισμὸς πολύς, οἱ δὲ ἐργάται ὀλίγοι· δεήθητε οὖν τοῦ κυρίου τοῦ
θερισμοῦ ὅπως ἐκβάλῃ ἐργάτας εἰς τὸν θερισμὸν αὐτοῦ – should
perhaps be interpreted in the sense that the disciples were being invited to
pray to God so that he would make even more of those who heard Jesus'
message disposed to obey his concrete call to follow him, so that they
might in this way be placed in the service of proclaiming the nearness of
the rule of God. The authenticity of this saying is made probable by the
fact that in the later community tradition the harvest no longer appears as
a figure for the Mission. Here the harvest rather becomes a metaphor –
as it already was in the prophets and apocalyptic literature – for the
judgement, and the harvesters are not the messengers of the Mission, but
the angels.[143] 'But for Jesus the harvest-time has already arrived, because
the rule of God is dawning.'[144] Jn 4.35 may also be a further development
of our logion.[145]

R. Tarphon's motto (end of first century A.D.) which is in a way
related to this again shows the radical difference from Jesus' message despite all its formal points of contact: 'the day is short, the
work is great, the workers are lazy. The reward is great and the
master of the house is pressing' (Ab 2.15). The shortness of the time
and pressure from the householder refer here not to the nearness of
God's rule but to the brevity of human life, and the 'work' does not
consist in 'mission' – as 2.16 shows – but in intensive preoccupa-
tion with the Torah. This receives its due reward: 'If you have
learned much Torah, you will be given a great reward'.

In the Mission tradition itself the Q version – which in its individual
features is, moreover, relatively more rigorous[146] – reveals itself as the

---

[142] F. Hahn, op.cit. (n.138), 32. Cf. also H. D. Wendland, op.cit. (n.137), 156f.

[143] On mission conceived in terms of planting and building see 1 Cor 3.6ff., 10ff. On the
'harvest' as a picture of judgment see Mt 13.30, 39 (for the angels as workers in the harvest
cf. Mk 13.27//s) and Rev 14.15. Cf. also Joel 4.13; Jer 50 (LXX 27),16 and Is 18.4ff.; 2 Esd
4.28ff., 35; 9.17; syr Bar 70.2; slav En 42 11 vs. B.

[144] F. Hahn, loc. cit. (n.138), 32. Cf. J. Jeremias, op.cit. (n.40), 118f. (E.T. 119f.) and C.
H. Dodd, *The Parables of the Kingdom*, 2nd ed., 1961, 143f.

[145] Op.cit. 32 n.1 and 142.

[146] Cf. Mk 6.8 with Lk 10.4 and Mt 10.9f. According to the Q tradition, even sandals and a
staff are forbidden, this in contrast to the later, Markan form. The disciples' lack of needs
thus acquires an almost parabolic character. As such a tradition contradicts the actual
mission requirements of the post-Easter period, it is hardly conceivable as a community-
formation. Consequently Mark is an attenuation although the equipment of the messen-

original. According to F. Hahn, its climax comes 'in the commission to proclaim God's rule and to act with authority'. Even if in Q the composition of the Mission instruction as a whole probably represents the work of the early Palestinian community, the 'demand to go forth without any equipment is' nevertheless 'completely compatible with Jesus' attitude in its radical nature and in its parallelism to the sayings on "following" him which likewise demand renunciation of all possessions of one's own'. There is all the more reason, therefore, 'to regard as genuine the commission to proclaim, as Jesus himself did, the approach of God's rule, and like him to perform acts of power but also where appropriate to execute a curse'.[147]

This picture is filled out by the unique, enigmatic saying that follows Peter and Andrew's call: 'Follow me, and I shall make you fishers of men!' (δεῦτε ὀπίσω μου, καὶ ποιήσω ὑμᾶς γενέσθαι ἁλεεῖς ἀνθρώπων Mk 1.17//) whose differently worded parallel tradition in Lk 5.10: ἀπὸ τοῦ νῦν ἀνθρώπους ἔσῃ ζωγρῶν, representing a translation variant, is sufficient ground for positing an underlying Aramaic logion.[148] The saying can be translated back into Hebrew and Aramaic without difficulty; confirmation of the translation can be provided from the Old Testament and the Targums. The peculiar difference between Mk 1.17 and Lk 5.10 can be explained by the fact that in the post-biblical period 'sayyad' could mean both 'hunter' and 'fisherman'. By way of comparison we may add the Peshitta version to our attempt at retranslation.[148a]

---

gers, without a knapsack, is still inferior to that of the wandering Cynic preacher (see above, p.27f.). Is Jesus to be thought of as having, on sending out his disciples, made a similar demand to that made, according to Ber 9.5, in connection with walking on the Temple mount without staff or sandals, or money pouch (TBer 7.19 p.17)? In this case we should have before us a genuine parabolic action. H. Schürmann gives a divergent analysis of the tradition about the sending out of the disciples in *Neutestamentliche Aufsätze J. Schmid*, 1963, 270-282. He sees in Lk 10.1, in Mt 10.5b, 6 and in Lk 10.8-11 the 'core and the main element of the entire *pericope* about the sending out of the disciples', and he considers that this *pericope* will go back to Jesus' 'act of sending them out' (281).

[147] F. Hahn, op.cit. (n.138), 32, 34.

[148] According to K. Beyer, *Semitische Syntax im NT*, SUNT 1 (1962) I. 1.252 the connection of imperative + kai + future in Mk 1.17 = Mt 4.19 very probably points to 'Semitic influence'.

[148a] See M. Jastrow, *Dictionary*, 2.1276a: 'hunter, fowler, fisher'; cf. C. Brockelmann, *Lexicon Syriacum*, 627: sajjādā, 'venator . . . piscator'. This 'attempt at retranslation' is in no way an attempt to reconstruct a '*verbum ipsissimum*' of Jesus, but only to buttress the Palestinian origin of the logion, which has been repeatedly contested. I am using here a method such as has been effectively tried out in our working groups in Aramaic at Tübingen under the leadership of Dr Rüger. (a) 2 Kings 6.19 M and Tg; (b) cf. Ex 32.10; Num 14.12; Deut 9.14; see also Gen 12.2 and 2 Sam 7.9b; (c) cf. 4QTest 24 (Lohse, 250): 'someone from Belial appears, to become a net for his people' אחד בליעל עומד להיות פוח יוקוש לעמו; further, 2 Sam 7.8b; 1 Kings 1.35; 1 Chron 28.4; 2 Chron 6.5. On the translation of להיות by γενέσθαι see Jer 13.11 and Ezek 17.14; (d) cf. Jer 16.16; on the twofold possibility see the *parallelismus membrorum* in 2 Sam 7.14; (e) 1QH 5.8 offers another form.

d   c   b   a

בְּנֵי אָדָם

לְכוּ אַחֲרַי וְאֶעֱשֶׂה אֶתְכֶם לְ(הִיוֹת) צַיָּדֵי אֲנָשִׁים

צַיָּדִים לִבְנֵי אָדָם

אֵיתוֹ בָּתְרַי וְאֶעֱבֵד יָתְכוֹן / לְ(מֶהֱוֵי) צַיָּדֵי בְּנֵי אֲנָשָׁא

ܠܗ ܚܠܐܬ ܘܐܚܕܝܗܡ ܪܝܡܐ ܘܚܒܐ ܐܢܗܐ

We can hardly cite against the genuineness of this figure of speech the
fact that it has no known direct rabbinical parallels. Surely we will have to
allow Jesus to have coined some original sayings of his own! It is equally
perverse to think that the whole anecdote in Mk 1.16, 17 has been 'spun
out of' this saying.[149] The figure occurs several times in negative form in
the Old Testament and above all at Qumran, where we read of fishermen
spreading their nets (against the sons) of iniquity, and of the three nets of
Belial;[150] in the Greek tradition we find it in predominantly negative
form.[151] Reversing its use at Qumran, might we not interpret the figure
positively, to mean that under the auspices of the dawning rule of God
and as commissioned by their master, the disciples were intended – like
Jesus himself – to deprive the 'strong man' (see above p.65f.) of his booty
and to free those who were bound (Lk 13.16 cf.4.18)? We can hardly say

[149] E. Haenchen's supposition in *Weg Jesu*, 81, that the word 'has no counterpart in the
Semitic', will not hold water. Likewise R. Bultmann's supposition in *Syn. Trad.* 27 (E.T. 28)
lacks any foundation ('the scene . . . has been spun out of the metaphor which was already to
hand'). Such a saying, lacking a setting, could scarcely be handed on, as it would be
meaningless.

[150] Cf. Jer 16.16: ἰδοὺ ἐγὼ ἀποστέλλω τοὺς ἁλεεῖς τοὺς πολλούς... καὶ ἁλιεύσουσιν
αὐτοὺς καί... τοὺς πολλοὺς θηρευτὰς καὶ θηρεύσουσιν αὐτούς; Prov. 6.26b: γυνὴ δὲ
ἀνδρῶν τιμίας ψυχὰς ἀγρεύει cf. also Ezek 13.18 (M). On the Qumran texts see 1QH 5.8
which follows Jer 16.16: 'staying as a stranger with many fishers who spread a net over the
water and (with) hunters for the sons of wickedness'. Cf. 1QH 3.26, the drag-net of the
godless or 2.29. On Belial's net, see CD 4.15f. cf. TDan 2.4. For a rabbinic tradition see in
Bill 1.188: Rome as the catcher of human beings. Cf. C. W. F. Smith, HThR 52 (1959), 187
and O. Betz RQ 3 (1961), 53ff. where there is a series of further, related references.

[151] The parallel quoted in the commentaries (see E. Klostermann, Mk, HNT 1950 4th
ed., 12f.; E. Lohmeyer, Mk, MeyerK 1953 12th ed., 32 n.4; E. Haenchen, *Weg Jesu*, 81 n.9,
cf. also W. Bauer, *Wörterbuch z. NT*, 1958 5th ed., 74 (E.T. 37)) from a mediaeval
gnomological manuscript, see J. Freudenthal, RhMus NF 35 (1880), 413 n.12 is a very late
exegetical and so secondary version of Diog Laert 2.67 who rightly ascribes it to Aristippus
and not, like the collection of sayings, to Solon. Athen 12.544d, provides a third version. As
the concept of 'fishing for men' appears neither in Diogenes Laertius nor in Athenaeus, the
secondary version could for its part have been influenced by Mk 1.17. It will not be necessary
to lay great weight upon it. On the other hand, the related verb θηρᾶν is used twice
figuratively in Diog Laert 4.16f (and Jer 16.16 and 1QH 5.8 also link fishermen and hunters),
(see above p.28, on Xenocrates and Polemo), and 8.36, Timon on Pythagoras: θήρη ἐπ'
ἀνθρώπων = 'a hunter of men'. On the Lukan version with ζωγρεῖν see W. Bauer, op.cit.
672 (E.T. 340) and cf. with 2 Tim 2.26: καὶ ἀνανήψωσιν ἐκ τῆς τοῦ διαβόλου παγίδος
ἐζωγρημένοι ὑπ' αὐτοῦ as in the Qumran texts the devil appears here as the 'catcher of
men'.

in the mutually exclusive sense 'that Jesus . . . saw himself as sent not to
fight the devil but to serve mankind',[152] for there was no contrast between
these two notions in Jesus' mind or in that of the primitive community,
but rather a manifestation in men of the victory over the prince of evil: in
this sense service of the Kingdom (Basileia) was, for the disciples too,
equally and unreservedly 'service of mankind'. However we are to understand this saying in detail, one thing is certain from consideration of its
parallels in the Old Testament, Qumran, and the Greek 'diatribe': in
general linguistic usage it had a predominantly negative ring, meaning
more or less 'those who trap men' or 'slave stealers' – comparable with
the Greek term ἀνδραποδιστής. It may therefore well be that behind it
lay a paradoxical and provocative logion of Jesus' which might be compared with the saying about the 'dead who bury their dead'. G. Klein's
attempt to demonstrate that Luke's version is the more original comes to
grief because Jesus' reply in Lk 5.10 reveals itself – with the exception of
the translation variant ἀνθρώπους . . . ζωγρῶν which comes from the
tradition – as a clearly Lukan formulation which matches Luke's view of
the simultaneous nature of the call to follow Jesus and the call to missionary proclamation. Furthermore there does not seem to be much point in
linking with Peter's resurrection a saying which has such a provocative
and offensive undertone. And because of the saying's originality there is
little probability in the idea that this is later community formulation from
a Palestinian environment. Whether addressed in the plural to the two
brothers or in the singular to Peter alone the formulation points back to
Jesus himself.[152a]

If the disciple in following Jesus was to share the same mission and
authority as Jesus himself, he likewise needed to be free for this service,
unrestrictedly ready to share the total insecurity, exposure to danger, and
slander which were the fate of his master: 'The pupil is not above the
teacher, or the slave above his master. It is sufficient for the pupil to be
like his teacher and for the slave to be like his master. If they have called

---

[152] E. Käsemann EVuB 1.208 (E.T. 39f.). The struggle against the 'strong man' (Mt
12.29//, see above p.66) does not mean that Jesus shared the ideas of a 'metaphysical
dualism' of the Essene type. See on this H. Braun, *Qumran u. d. NT*, 2.96f.: 'Qumran
displays a fully developed system of basic dualism, . . . On the other hand Jesus' miracles of
healing imply a popular demonism, not worked out in dualistic terms'. We find this request,
for example, in an apocryphal Psalm of David from 11Q, which has decidedly 'wisdom'-type
features: 'Let not Satan rule over me nor an unclean spirit, nor should pain and the evil
inclination possess my bones' DJDJ IV 771.15f. (see above, n.38). Here we have an example
of a popular, pre-Essene demonism.

[152a] See G. Klein, ZNW 58 (1967), 1-44, esp. 12ff. On the Lukan character of μὴ φοβοῦ
see 1.13, 30; 5.10; 8.50; 12.32; Acts 18.9; 27.24: it is a well-established, characteristic Lukan
formula. By contrast, Mt does not have it at all and Mk has it only once, in the traditional
formulation of 5.36. On the temporal phrase ἀπὸ τοῦ νῦν, see Lk 1.48; 5.10; 12.52; 22.18, 69
and Acts 18.6. Again it is found in Mt and Mk. On the linking of calling and 'mission' see Lk
9.60b (on which see above p.4 n.4), the double mission in 9.1ff. and 10.1ff. and, further,
the shepherds in 2.17 and Paul in Acts 9.19ff.

the master of the house Beezebul, how much more will they malign those of his household.'[153]

To this linking of the *call to follow Jesus with the commissioning and Mission* of his disciples it cannot reasonably be objected that in the Gospels the activity of the disciples falls wholly into the background over against that of Jesus. It was rather almost inevitable that this bias should appear within the tradition, for the person of Jesus had, as a result of the crucifixion and the Easter event, become the absolute guarantor of salvation and from then on constituted the focal point of the primitive Christian kerygma, Jesus being regarded as the exalted Lord who would come again. The person and activity of the disciples as they followed their Master had by contrast no 'soteriological' dignity, and could not but fall into the background, for the community wished to be informed not about the 'words and deeds' of the first disciples but purely and solely about the activities of their Lord. Where the disciples were in fact mentioned by name the tradition told first and foremost of their lack of understanding and their failure.[154] The later Gospel tradition's reintroduction of the disciples more forcefully as individuals who talk and act happens only in order to make the *doxa* of the Kyrios radiate even more brightly. The Fourth Gospel provides us with the best example of this. From a historical standpoint what the community said in unfavourable reports on the disciples' behaviour may well be justified. It is quite likely that at least in part the disciples misunderstood Jesus' activity and mission, reading them, as did the mass of his Galilean audience, in terms of traditional Jewish national messianic hopes.[155] It is therefore entirely possible that because the disciples were caught up in apocalyptic and national notions, the service he had in mind for them as their specific personal vocation, was as a whole ineffective. Here of course it is difficult to pass beyond mere speculation. Nor, finally do we know anything certain about the duration of Jesus' activities till he was put to death. To my mind we must not put too long a period on it. To hazard a comparison, it had a

---

[153] Mt 10.24f. cf. Jn 13.16 and Lk 6.40, which of course destroys the *parallelismus membrorum*. Mt 10.25b has probably been added, but might nevertheless go back to an older logion, see R. Bultmann, *Synopt. Trad.*, 94 (E.T. 90). Cf. also above p.43f. nn. 21/22. On the logion itself see F. Hahn, op.cit. (p.4 n.4), 78 (E.T. 76). It is connected with the Jewish 'law on messengers'.

[154] Mk 8.16f.//; 8.32f.//s; 9.14, 18, 28, 33ff.//s; 10.13//s; 10.35-45//; 14.10f.//s; 14.28f.//s, and frequently. Naturally the disciples' failure is also a familiar theme in the tradition, see above p.26f. n.38 on Apollonius of Tyana. But this is in no way to imply that these reports are entirely unhistorical. If we can speak of a 'misunderstanding' of Jesus (see above p.39f.) this also concerns primarily the disciples. G. Klein's attempt to explain the undoubted difficulties in the traditions about Peter's denial in terms of a late polemical formation, leads to explaining what is obscure *per obscurius*, see ZThK 58 (1961), 258-328; cf. also E. Linnemann, ZThK 63 (1966), 1ff., 10f., 31f., who does at least hold to the fact of the disciples' failure especially in the Passion.

[155] See above p.40 nn.9, 10; cf. also 91. Cf. also E. Jüngel, *Paulus u. Jesus*, HUTh 2 (1962 = 1964 2nd ed.), 132 following E. Fuchs.

comet-like quality, suddenly blazing into view and with an even more sudden, hard and bitter end.[156] The revolutionary power of Jesus' message could hardly have made it possible for him to remain peaceably at work over a period of several years. Possibly there was no longer much time left for more intensive activities by the disciples really to develop along the lines we have indicated. At all events, quite apart from these problems, which are historically insoluble, the pressing proximity of God's rule itself did not leave any time for the development of a teacher-pupil relationship and for scholarly studies in the rabbinic fashion.

10 Jesus as the Teacher of his Disciples, and the Beginning of the Synoptic tradition

Nor do we know so very much about the way in which Jesus was himself the *teacher* of his disciples.[157] Direct evidence of specific instructions to the disciples as such is hard to provide, but such instruction might most plausibly be held to occur where we have Jesus rejecting false opinions and claims from them.[158] It is hardly likely in the light of the openness of his message as a whole that Jesus would to any great extent have given esoteric secret teaching.[159] The direct proximity of God, the 'last hour,' required not withdrawal from the world but open preaching which everyone could hear.[160] Nor do we anywhere find a demand for learning by rote and memorizing. When God's rule is at the gates there ceases to be any point in creating a tradition. What then counts is no longer learning but

[156] On the impossibility of a 'chronology' of Jesus' activity, see H. Conzelmann, RGG 3rd ed., 3.642ff. (E.T. *Jesus* 20ff.).

[157] On this see K. H. Rengstorf, ThW 2.155 (E.T. 2.155) and in disagreement with him E. Fascher, 'Jesus der Lehrer,' ThLZ 79 (1954), 325-342, who rightly stresses the difference from the rabbinical world, but does not separate the Synoptic and Johannine tradition and consequently overlooks the eschatological limitations of Jesus' message. See also A. Schulz, op.cit. (p.1 n.1), 56-62, who stresses that 'a reference to Jesus' instructing his disciples (is) . . . one of the most frequent ways of setting the scene employed by the editors' (58).

[158] Cf. e.g. Mk 8.14ff.//; 9.33ff.//s; 10.35-45//; 13.1ff.//s. The prophecies of the Passion should also be included here. The editorial hand of the Evangelist and certain stages in the formation of the tradition do of course show up in all these passages, but this is still not to say that they could not have had some kind of basis in Jesus' activity; see E. Schweizer, *Neotestamentica*, 1963, 96.

[159] J. Jeremias, op.cit. (n.116), 11ff. (E.T. 16ff.), supposes that in the period after Peter's confession Jesus turned away from the people and towards esoteric teaching of his disciples (14) (E.T. 18). Cf. also J. Gnilka, *Die Verstockung Israels*, StANT 3 (1961), 204f.; A. Schulz (p.1 n.1), 59 and 72. It is true that in Mk particularly between 8.27 and 10.52 the esoteric features do receive special emphasis, prior to Jesus' final activity, suffering and death in Jerusalem, see e.g. 9.30f.: in journeying through Galilee, 'he did not wish anyone to know of it. *For he was teaching his disciples*'. However, as the Markan framework does not have a biographical character, it would be difficult to demonstrate such a development in Jesus' preaching.

[160] Cf. Mt 10.26f. = Lk 12.2f. and E. Käsemann, EVuB 1.209 (E.T. 40-42) on this. Jn 18.20f. (cf. Mk 14.49//s), which is apologetically formulated, also emphasizes the public nature of Jesus' preaching.

obedience in action. The controversy which was always troubling the
rabbis, about whether learning the Torah or doing it was the more
important, stands thus in complete and irreconcilable contrast to Jesus'
message.[161]

Here we might ask how then it came about that the tradition of Jesus'
words and deeds was preserved at all – particularly when nowhere is
there anything said in the Gospels about the disciples' 'learning' a special
halakah of Jesus – seeing that after all the royal rule of God did not dawn
ἐν δυνάμει but that instead Jesus was crucified and the disciples were
scattered? In answer we must point to the way in which the receptive
memory of Jesus' disciples, who of course – in contrast to the masses –
heard him constantly, was given excellent assistance by the well-defined,
figurative form of the pronouncements, parables and pictorial sayings in
which Jesus couched his teaching in order to leave a lasting impression on
his audience. But the relative *smallness* of the units in which almost
without exception the 'preaching' of Jesus has come down to us in the
Synoptic tradition might also be regarded as an indication that the disciples simply did not subject what they heard to intensive memoriza-
tion – in contrast to the Mishnah and Gemara where everything
depended on the scholar's careful memorizing of as large complexes of
systematically arranged material as possible.[162]

The conscious goal after which the disciples who 'followed' Jesus strove
was simply not, as with the rabbis, to carry on the tradition or to create a
new tradition, but *to prepare for the service of the approaching rule of
God.* This occurred in the constant sharing of their lives with the master,
and preeminently in their repeated hearing of his preaching to the people.
No scholarly accessories were needed! To my mind this intention is
clearly expressed in the introduction to the appointment of the 'Twelve'
in Mk 3.13f.:

> And he went up on the mountain and called to him *those whom he
> desired,* and they came to him. And he made twelve, *to be with him,*
> and to be *sent out* to preach, and have authority to cast out evil
> spirits: καὶ προσκαλεῖται οὓς ἤθελεν αὐτός, καὶ ἀπῆλθον πρὸς
> αὐτόν. καὶ ἐποίησεν δώδεκα ἵνα ὦσιν μετ' αὐτοῦ, καὶ ἵνα
> ἀποστέλλῃ αὐτοὺς κηρύσσειν καί ἔχειν ἐξουσίαν ἐκβάλλειν τὰ
> δαιμόνια.

Even if the Evangelists' editorial hand can be clearly traced here, the
meaning and purpose of the call of the disciples is entirely faithfully
reproduced in this summary, though admittedly the number of disciples
called by Jesus to the 'service of the Kingdom' is probably not to be
limited to the Twelve.[163] This would also lend decisive weight to H. E.

---

[161] See Bill 3.85ff. and 1.467, 469. Cf. on the other hand the 'hearing and doing' of Lk 6.47
= Mt 7.24.   [162] See B. Gerhardsson, *Memory,* 123-170.
[163] R. Bultmann's view, *Syn. Trad.,* 369 (E.T. 345), that Mk always meant this, even

Tödt's significant thesis that the Q source basically represents the continued proclamation of Jesus' message, related to the current circumstances of the community.[164] Purely hypothetically we might ask whether the process of the development of a tradition of the Logia of Jesus, including even the stylization of individual anecdotes, did not in fact have its first beginnings – albeit quite unintentionally – during Jesus' lifetime in the Mission of the disciples, always remembering that this Mission may not have been a unique event.[165] The disciples were not instructed to reproduce Jesus' message as literally as possible, so that this may be the reason for the relatively early, almost inseparable fusion of their own material and Logia of Jesus. And if this process had already begun – even if only for a short time – while Jesus himself was still active, we would have an explanation for the relative freedom with which from the start the missionary Palestinian community linked up with the transmission of Jesus' Logia what *they themselves* had to say about the situation in the shape of statements that arose out of their link with the exalted Lord. For even if Jesus' authority had become without qualification an absolute authority as a result of its being divinely confirmed by the Resurrection, there was no feeling of being slavishly tied tó the exact wording of the individual Logia, for his followers were directly linked with him through the Spirit and awaited his return in the near future. Even then there was still no intention to form a tradition in the strict rabbinic sense. From this perspective the Jewish-Christian scribal school which we find in Matthew is a relatively late phenomenon.

The office of an *'apostle'* too would not then have to be derived either from 'Gnosis' or from the rabbinical institution of the *šalîaḥ* but would in the nature of the case go back to Jesus' call and sending out of the disciples and would represent the actual fruit of Jesus' call to follow him. The question of the origins of the *title* 'apostle' would by comparison be secondary, and here the real prototype – as for the call of the disciples –

before the appointment of the Twelve, is improbable (2.15f., 18, 23; 3.7, 9). Such a measure of literary naïvety can hardly be credited to Mk; rather does he deliberately increase the number of disciples, see 1.16f., 29; 2.13, 15; ἦσαν γὰρ πολλοί, καὶ ἠκολούθουν αὐτῷ see V. Taylor, *St Mark*, 1966, 2nd ed., 205 in loc.; cf. also W. G. Kümmel, HuG 291 n.10: even later it is not always without exception the Twelve who are intended. See also J. Roloff, *Apostolat...* , 1965, 138ff.

[164] *Menschensohn*, 225-231 (E.T. 246-254).

[165] H. Schürmann makes an effort in this direction in 'Die vorösterlichen Anfänge der Logientradition', in H. Ristow and K. Matthiae op.cit. (n.3), 342-370, though of course he overestimates the possibility of a stabilising of the tradition of the logia, which is said to have had its 'Sitz im Leben', in the 'pre-Easter' preaching situation (363f.). The thesis that Jesus 'formed his logia deliberately and passed them on (sic) to his disciples to put them in possession of aids for their own preaching' (362) seems to me to go much too far. Nevertheless it is basically necessary to take into account the possibility that because of his sending disciples out on a mission the formation of logia did already germinate in Jesus' circle of disciples, even if no direct didactic intentions can be demonstrated for Jesus in this respect. However we must on no account overlook the fact that Jesus is nowhere recorded in the tradition as having urged his disciples to 'learn' his sayings, see above p.51.

would appear to be the call of the Old Testament prophets where the verb שלח (= ἀποστέλλειν LXX) repeatedly plays a fundamental role.[166] One cannot therefore see why this title should not have already emerged in Palestine even prior to Paul, the more so as the so-called 'Hellenistic community' clearly has its roots in Palestine – in fact, in Jerusalem itself. In Jesus' day Palestine was a country where two or rather three languages were spoken. This can be gathered not only from the huge numbers of Greek inscriptions from Jewish Palestine in New Testament times but also from the language of rabbinic literature, which is interlarded with Greek loan-words.[167] P. Stuhlmacher has similarly shown the Palestinian derivation of the terms בִּשֵּׂר = εὐαγγελίξεσθαι and בְּשׂוֹרָה = εὐαγγέλιον in primitive Christianity.[168]

A further point seems significant. Perhaps the very fact that there is an almost inseparable fusion of the 'Jesus tradition' and 'community formations' in the Gospel-traditions of the sending out of the disciples may be taken to imply that there was in a special way a conscious awareness at this point of the 'continuity' between Jesus' activity and the later activities of the community. Thus we must not always understand the diagnostic terms 'community formation' on the lips of the researcher only to imply a great gap from the historical Jesus. The community's freedom under the guidance of the prophetic spirit is something which, visible as it is in such 'community formations', could also be an expression of the fact that the community was aware of being particularly close to the historical Jesus in action, which was the starting point for its own missionary proclamation. This line could be extended to Paul. Consciously or unconsciously, when he says of himself and Apollos in 1 Cor 3.9: θεοῦ γάρ ἐσμεν συνεργοί – or even more pointedly in 2 Cor 5.20: ὑπὲρ Χριστοῦ οὖν πρεσβεύομεν ὡς τοῦ θεοῦ παρακαλοῦντος δι' ἡμῶν – Paul stands directly in the line of that event which Jesus had inaugurated by his call to follow him and by his sending out the disciples in mission.

[166] Ex 3.10-15; Is 6.8; Ezek 2.4; cf. also 1Sam 15.1; Jer 19.14; 25.17; 26.12; Ezek 13.6 and frequently. The rabbis too were familiar with the idea of men endowed with charismatic authority who were distinguishable by their miracles, which were reserved for God alone to do, see K. H. Rengstorf, ThW 1.419 (E.T. 1.417ff.).

[167] See M. Hengel, op.cit. (p.27 n.41), 75ff.; 141ff.

[168] P. Stuhlmacher, *Das Paulinische Evangelium. I. Vorgeschichte*, 1968. passim.

IV Conclusion

1 Comments on a new study of the meaning of 'following' Jesus

Taking as our starting-point the saying about 'following' in Mt 8.21f = Lk 9.59f. we have tried to solve the problem of the origin and meaning of the call of individual disciples to follow Jesus. Given the limited scope of this study, the result can only be provisional. Nevertheless we believe that we come some way towards the problem's solution. We have quite deliberately eschewed a more comprehensive discussion of the varied manifestations of the idea of 'following' in the four Gospels, and have directed our enquiries to the meaning of the call to 'follow' for Jesus himself. This distinguishes the present investigation in principle from the latest work on the subject by H. D. Betz, who basically passes over the question of the meaning of the call of the disciples and of 'following' for the historical Jesus and attempts to sketch 'the interpretation of "following" Jesus in the Gospels' only in the barest outline;[1] this done, he moves without delay to a far more detailed treatment of the idea of *mimesis* (imitation) in the ancient, and particularly in the Greek world.[2] Nevertheless the central feature of Synoptic research must continue to be the attempt to get back to Jesus himself. Neither the approach of redaction-criticism, currently so popular, nor form-critical endeavours can or ought to replace this. We must not forget that our knowledge of primitive Christian history up to the completion of the Gospels is certainly no greater than our knowledge of Jesus himself, even where it is based on a critical reading of the sources. The question mark suspended over the

[1] *Nachfolge und Nachahmung Jesu Christi im Neuen Testament,* BHTh 37 (1967), 27-43.

[2] Op.cit., 48-136: This is where the author is revealed in his true colours. He consequently believes that already in Mk 'following Jesus approximated in structural terms to mystery' (dem Mysterienhaften). Unfortunately the term 'mystery' (mysterienhaft), which is frequently used by him, remains substantially unclear; see on this 146 n.4 and, contrary to it, G. Delling, ThW 8.70 (E.T. 8.73); 154: on 1 Cor 4.16 and Paul as a 'Christian mystagogue'; 156: ὁδός as a 'term belonging to the mysteries'; the term is used endlessly in the Judaism of the period in a figurative way; 172: Paul's thought is 'structurally not gnostic, but is nevertheless . . . closely related to mystery (wohl aber . . . mysterienhaft) cf. 173, 176, 183, 185. Unfortunately he does not tell us what he really means by 'mysterious in character' (mysterienhaft), and similarly he hardly quotes any linguistic parallels. On this somewhat 'mysterious' − not to say mystifying − use of language I can only point to the considered verdict of U. v. Wilamowitz-Moellendorf, *Der Glaube der Hellenen,* 1959, 3rd ed., 2.381: 'these hypothetical mysteries appear to me to be wishful thinking, . . . deriving certain expressions and teachings of Paul from anywhere, because Judaism is not adequate as a source. There is some justification for the wish, but to invent a "mystery religion" does not fulfill that wish for anyone who demands items of evidence'. Cf. H. Langerbeck, *Aufs. z. Gnosis,* AGG 1967, 84ff.

chronological development of the tradition in the period of roughly forty years between 30 and 70 A.D. – i.e. till the Gospel of Mark came into being – should draw our attention to the fact that frequently in the exercise of our judgment, we explain what is relatively well known to us by what is a great deal less well-known, when we dissolve well-attested tradition in the Synoptic Gospels in the anonymous 'community tradition'. Strangely enough, the more scepticism about the Synoptic tradition develops into radicalism of the extremist kind, the greater is the tendency to indulge in imaginative hypotheses with regard to the history of primitive Christianity. One might well question whether this process should be equated with genuine progress of a scholarly kind. Thus, when on the specific linguistic usage of the Synoptics H. D. Betz roundly declares 'that ἀκολουθεῖν goes back to the oldest stratum only in a few places, and that most of the references belong to secondary legends (call-narratives), editorial seams and miracle stories' without providing any evidence for this, and then proceeds directly to deal with the later development of the notion in Q and the four Gospels[3] he is obfuscating rather than illuminating the historical picture. The astonished reader, who was led by the rather ambitious title '*Nachfolge und Nachahmung Jesu Christi im Neuen Testament*' (*Following and Imitating Jesus Christ in the New Testament*) to expect rather more in the way of instruction would indeed be grateful for illumination on how the idea of 'following' came to be developed by Jesus or by those who came after him. The point Betz makes – which is neither immune from contradiction nor new – 'The idea of following Jesus is rooted in the Palestinian Jewish relationship of the teacher of the Torah to his pupil' – is taken over as an unexamined axiom[4] and appears no more credible for the added qualification that 'in the Gospels, however, it has become an independent variation'. The author, it is true, rightly recognizes that this traditional explanation of Jesus' call to follow him places the 'historian' in a 'dilemma', but he deduces only two possibilities from this: either one finds an escape from the dilemma in the radical scepticism which says that 'the picture of Jesus "calling" disciples is entirely secondary', or else one supposes – in a way which for him can no longer be substantiated – 'that Jesus' disciples must have had a relationship to their master for which Judaism provides us with no analogies'. Thus he steers only with difficulty between Scylla and Charybdis, i.e. between destructive scepticism and postulates he cannot verify, and reaches this somewhat vague compromise: 'The idea that . . . Jesus called disciples will therefore *not* be an *entirely* secondary construction, but the fact that Jesus had disciples will have to be supplemented by the assumption that he gave his own special stamp to this discipleship, just as being a disciple of John the Baptist or being a member of the Qumran Community in each case had its own special characteristics'.[5] It is in vain that one

---

[3] H. D. Betz, op.cit. 27, cf. 10.   [4] Op.cit. 3; cf. 11.
[5] Op.cit. 11, 13; (my italics).

tries to go beyond this extremely general remark in the search for a characterization of these 'special characteristics' supported by the texts of the Gospels. One is given instead only a very limited selection of the modern discussion on the historical Jesus and his disciples.[6] By contrast the origin of the idea of 'following' remains in obscurity and only later does one again come up against the – quite marginal – point 'that, in primitive Palestinian Christianity, the idea of following after Christ – filled with new content – arose from the relationship of master and pupil among the rabbis',[7] which is a misleading statement, since it ignores the fact that there is no bridge from the rabbinate to following Jesus. The enigma of what Jesus' call to follow him originally meant remains unsolved. Here we come up against a phenomenon which is increasingly discernible; radical methodical scepticism leads to its being possible basically to utter only general commonplaces about the historical Jesus. This of course could have the grave consequence that we would lose altogether the criteria for differentiating Jesus from certain highly questionable religious figures of his age and environment.

2 Survey in retrospect

The Synoptic sources do not justify such a comprehensive and hence to my mind uncritical scepticism. As to the subject we have been considering we may rather say that the criteria for a well-founded enquiry into the Jesus of history, which have been sharply delineated by Käsemann, are particularly applicable here: Jesus' call to follow him can 'neither be derived from Judaism nor ascribed to primitive Christianity'.[8] Here we must start from the fact that the tradition about 'following after' him is already to be found in formed units of tradition in both Mark and Q, independently of each other. These units, for their part, point back to the primitive community in Palestine. However it is impossible that this was where for the first time there occurred the free development of this whole complex of ideas, including the link of the verb 'follow after' with the phenomenon of personal attachment to Jesus in the sense of an unqualified community of destiny. It is impossible, because it would have seemed absurd to emphasize the term 'walking behind' in relation to the exalted Son of Man. The idea was intelligible only if applied to an actual human being. It is no accident that – with one exception – the specific application of the word in the New Testament is confined to the earthly Jesus.[9]

[6] Op.cit. 13-27.
[7] Op.cit. 139; following G. Kittel, ThW 1.213f. (E.T. 1.211ff.) who of course gives greater emphasis to the new content of the idea of 'following' by italicisation.
[8] EVuB 1.205 (E.T. 36f.); see on this the supplementary correction by W. G. Kümmel, ThR 31 (1965/66), 42f. cf. 43 n.1 Lit.
[9] Except for Rev 14.4 which comes from the Palestinian tradition. We first find a figurative sense in Ignatius, Philadelphians 2.1 and Smyrnans 8.1. To H. D. Betz's con-

Also, the Palestinian communities had better things to do than to copy in this point the usage of their Pharisaic opponents, who were among their sharpest critics – only to go on to change its meaning radically. This kind of reconstruction of the history of the term is hardly persuasive. Rather the phenomenon points back to Jesus himself. And as to Judaism, it is our hope that we have proved that Jesus' relationship to his disciples simply cannot be derived from the analogy of the teacher-pupil relationship such as we find it among the later rabbis. And, despite stronger points of contact with the apocalyptic prophets of his day than with the rabbis, Jesus is also fundamentally different from them too. Their aim was to gain the masses as their adherents, whereas he gathered only a few individuals directly around him. They led their followers across the Jordan into the desert to see the wonders of the eschatological exodus, he finally went to Jerusalem to confront the entire people with God's eschatological will, with the possibility of violent death staring him in the face. Neither the misleading term 'rabbi' nor the designation 'eschatological prophet', which is likewise open to misunderstanding, can adequately characterize his activity. Jesus' 'charisma' breaks through the possibilities of categorization in terms of the phenomenology of religion. The very uniqueness of the way in which Jesus called individuals to 'follow after' him is an expression of this underivable 'messianic' authority. We can therefore do nothing but agree with H. Conzelmann when he emphasizes that 'what is specific in Jesus' self-consciousness is documented in his relationship with his disciples'.[10] As this attitude of his was given its stamp by his messianic, eschatological mission, it would also be 'idle to ask how Jesus would have envisaged the relationship in the longer term'. With his disciples he is looking 'towards the nearness of the Kingdom' (l.c.). If we try to fathom even more precisely the enigma of the call to follow him and to be disciples, here too we stumble on the fact formulated – in another connection – by E. Fuchs, that Jesus' 'dared to act in God's place' (see above p.68). As to the call of the disciples, in the last analysis only the call of the Old Testament prophets by the God of Israel himself is a genuine analogy. Jesus' call is uttered with an eye to the dawning rule of God and he brings the individual person who is called by him into a community of life and destiny with him, involving an absolute break with all ties, thus at

---

clusion, op.cit. 139, that Paul never knew the term at all because he did not use it in accordance with Synoptic linguistic usage, it should be replied that he never was *able* to use it, because he had simply not been a 'follower' of the historical Jesus. In his situation the term 'imitation' in its different variations was on the other hand entirely appropriate. The astonishingly 'pregnant use' of ἀκολουθεῖν (see G. Kittel, ThW 1.214 (E.T. 1.214)) is to be explained only by the fact that it was originally firmly anchored in the activity of Jesus himself. This initially prevented its direct transfer to the relationship to the exalted Christ. See above p.62.

[10] RGG 3rd ed., 3.629 (E.T. 33-35 esp. 35). C. also emphasizes the basic difference from the rabbis. H. D. Betz, who in op.cit. 13 takes over H. Conzelmann's formulation, unfortunately does not make it very clear what *he himself* regards as the 'specific' element.

the same time initiating him into service for the cause of the Kingdom (Basileia). This gives the Mission tradition in Mk and Q its necessary and fully justified sense. The disciples were to act for the dawning Rule of God with the same authority as their master who called them. Only in the post-Easter community did 'following after' and discipleship become an expression of existence in faith, with the insistence that every believer is at the same time brought into the service of the Christ of God.

In this way, finally, one could explain the peculiar phenomenon, that, after the appearances of the risen Christ there began first the mission within Judaism and also, a few years later, the mission to the Samaritans and to the Gentiles, all of which constitutes a unique development for the eschatological movements within Judaism and for the ancient world in general. Even Jewish propaganda, which was the most active among the religions of the day, was quickly eclipsed by the eschatologically motivated misionary zeal of the primitive Christians. If, therefore, the Gospels partly projected the missionary situation of a later age back on to the activity of Jesus, this is not completely without justification even from a historical standpoint. There then also developed, parallel to the development of the missionary task – both to Jews and to Gentiles – and closely connected with it, the formation and shaping of the Jesus-tradition.[11] It might perhaps in its very earliest stages be connected with the sending forth of the disciples by Jesus himself. For both – i.e. for the primitive Christian mission and for the elaboration of the Jesus-tradition which then later found its deposit in the Gospels – the call by Jesus himself of individual disciples into the service of the dawning rule of God constitutes an initial point of departure.

[11] M. Dibelius, *Formgeschichte,* 12 (E.T. 13): 'The missionary purpose was the cause and preaching was the means of spreading abroad that which the disciples of Jesus possessed as recollections. We find traces of this still in 1 Cor 11.23ff.; 7.10; 9.14 (see also above, p.74 n.139a); 1 Thess 4.15 cf. 5.2 and I Cor 15.3-7.

List of Abbreviations

Ab	Pirqe Abot (Mishna tractate)
AGSU	Arbeiten zur Geschichte des Spätjudentums und Urchristentums
ALUOS	Annual of the Leeds University Oriental Society
ANET	Ancient Near Eastern Texts . . . (ed. J. B. Pritchard)
Ant	Josephus: Antiquitates
Anth Gr	Anthologia Graeca
ARN	Abot de Rabbi Natan
ASNU	Acta Seminarii Neotestamentici Upsaliensis
ASTI	Annual of the Swedish Theological Institute in Jerusalem, Leiden
ATh	Arbeiten zur Theologie
AThANT	Abhandlungen zur Theologie des Alten und Neuen Testaments
Athen	Athenaeus
AZ	Aboda Zara (Talmund tractate)
BAL	Berichte über die Verhandlungen der Sächsischen Akademie der Wissenschaften zu Leipzig
BB	Baba Batra (Talmud tractate)
Bell	Josephus: Bellum Judaicum
Ber	Berakhot (Talmud tractate)
BEvTh	Beiheft zu: Evangelische Theologie
BFCTh	Beiträge zur Förderung christlicher Theologie
BHTh	Beiträge zur Historischen Theologie
Bill	H. L. Strack u. P. Billerbeck: Kommentar zum NT aus Talmud und Midrasch
BJRL	Bulletin of the John Rylands Library
BM	Baba Meṣi'a (Talmud tractate)
BQ	Baba Qamma (Talmud tractate)
BSt	Biblische Studien
BZAW	Beihefte zur Zeitschrift für die alttestamentliche Wissenschaft
BZNW	Beihefte zur Zeitschrift für die neutestamentliche Wissenschaft
CantR	Canticum Rabba (Midrash on the Song of Songs)
Ḥag	Hagiga (Talmud tractate)
Ḥull	Hullin (Talmud tractate)
CIJ	Corpus Inscriptionum Judaicarum ed. J. B. Frey
CPJ	Corpus Papyrorum Judaicarum ed. Tcherikover-Fuks
dem ev	Euseb: Demonstratio Evangelica
Ed	Eduyot (Talmud tractate)
Erub	Erubin (Talmud tractate)
EsthR	Esther Rabba (Midrash on Esther)
ET	The Expository Times
EvTh	Evangelische Theologie
EVuB	E. Käsemann: Exegetische Versuche und Besinnungen
FRLANT	Forschungen zur Religion und Literatur des Alten und Neuen Testaments
GCS	Die Griechischen Christlichen Schriftsteller der ersten drei Jahrhunderte
GenR	Genesis Rabba (Midrash on Genesis)
Gitt	Giṭṭin (Talmud tractate)
HAT	Handbuch zum AT
HThR	Harvard Theological Review
HUCA	Hebrew Union College Annual
HuG	W. G. Kümmel: Heilsgeschehen und Geschichte

HUTh	Hermeneutische Untersuchungen zur Theologie
j	Jerusalem Talmud (Krotoschin edition)
JBL	Journal of Biblical Literature
Jos. a. Asen.	Joseph and Asenath
JvN	G. Bornkamm: Jesus von Nazareth
KAI	Donner-Röllig: Kanaanäische und Aramäische Inschriften
Keth	Kethubbot (Talmud tractate)
KohR	Kohelet Rabba (Midrash on Ecclesiastes)
LevR	Leviticus Rabba (Midrash on Leviticus)
LUA	Lunds Universitets Årsskrift
MBPAR	Münchener Beiträge zur Papyrusforschung u. antiken Rechtsgeschichte
MekEx	Mekilta zu Exodus (Tannaitic Midrash)
Meyer K	Krit.-exeget. Kommentar über das NT
MQ	Moed qaṭan (Talmud tractate)
Ned	Nedarim (Talmud tractate)
NovTest	Novum Testamentum
NTD	Das Neue Testament Deutsch
Pes	Pesaḥim (Talmud tractate)
PRE	Pirqe Rabbi Eliezer
PW	A. Pauly – G. Wissowa: Real-Encyclopädie der classischen Altertumswissenschaften
Qidd	Qiddushin (Talmud tractate)
RAC	Reallexikon für Antike und Christentum
RH	Rosh ha-shana (Talmud tractate)
RhMus	Rheinisches Museum für Philologie
RHPR	Revue d'Histoire et de Philosophie Religieuses
RQ	Revue de Qumrân
Sanh	Sanhedrin (Talmud tractate)
Shab	Shabbat (Talmud tractate)
Sheb	Shebuot (Talmud tractate)
Schürer	E. Schürer: Geschichte des Jüdischen Volkes im Zeitalter Jesu Christi, 3 Bde. 3. u. 4. ed. 1901-9.
SDtn	Sifre Deuteronomy (Tannaitic Midrash on Deuteronomy)
SNu	Sifre Numbers (Tannaitic Midrash on Numbers)
StANT	Studien zum Alten und Neuen Testament
StTh	Studia Theologica
SUNT	Studien zur Umwelt des Neuen Testament
SyBU	Symbolae Biblicae Uppsaliensis
T	Tosefta
Taan	Taanit (Talmud tractate)
Ter	Terumot (Talmud tractate)
TgJer I	Targum Jerusalem I
TgJon	Targum Jonathan (ben Uzziel)
TgO	Targum Onqelos
ThB	Theologische Bücherei
ThF	Theologische Forschung, Wissenschaftliche Beiträge zur kirchlich-evangelischen Lehre
ThHK	Theologischer Handkommentar zum NT
ThR	Theologische Rundschau
ThW	Theologisches Wörterbuch zum Neuen Testament
TU	Texte und Untersuchungen zur Geschichte der altchristlichen Literatur
UAC	E. Meyer, Ursprung und Anfänge des Christentums
UNT	Untersuchungen zum NT
UPZ	U. Wilcken, Urkunden der Ptolemäerzeit
WMANT	Wissenschaftliche Monographien zum Alten und Neuen Testament

WuD	Wort und Dienst. Jahrbuch der Theologischen Schule Bethel
WUNT	Wissenschaftliche Untersuchungen zum NT
ZDPV	Zeitschrift des Deutschen Palästina-Vereins
Zeb	Zebaḥim (Talmud tractate)
ZNW	Zeitschrift für die neutestamentliche Wissenschaft und die Kunde der älteren Kirche

English translations of German works referred to in the footnotes

Arndt & Gingrich, *A Greek-English Lexicon of the New Testament*, 1957
    (cf. W. Bauer, *Wörterbuch z. NT*, 1958, 5th ed.)

O. Betz, *What do we know about Jesus?*, 1968
    (cf. *Was wissen wir von Jesus?*, 1965)

G. Bornkamm, *Jesus of Nazareth*, 1960
    (cf. *Jesus von Nazareth*, 1959, 3rd ed.)

Bornkamm, Barth, Held, *Tradition and Interpretation in Matthew*, 1963
    (cf. *Ueberlieferung und Auslegung im Matthäeusevangelium*, 1960)

R. Bultmann, *Faith and Understanding*, 1966
    (cf. *Glauben und Verstehen*, I, 1933)
    History of the Synoptic Tradition, 1961
    (cf. *Geschichte der synoptischen Tradition*, 1931)
    Jesus and the Word, 1958
    (cf. *Jesus*, 1926)
    Primitive Christianity in its Contemporary Setting, 1956
    (cf. *Das Urchristentum im Rahmen der antiken Religionen*, 1962)
    Theology of the New Testament. 1952, 1955
    (cf. *Theologie des Neuen Testaments*, 1961, 4th ed.)

H. Conzelmann, *Jesus*, 1973
    (cf. *RGG* 3, 3rd ed.)
    The Theology of St Luke, 1960
    (cf. *Die Mitte der Zeit*, 1964, 5th ed.)

G. Dalman, *Jesus-Joshua*, 1929
    (cf. *Jesus-Jeschua*, 1922)

G. Dalman, *The Words of Jesus*
    (cf. *Die Worte Jesu*, 1930, 2nd ed.)

M. Dibelius, *From Tradition to Gospel*, 1934
    (cf. *Die Formgeschichte des Evangeliums*, 1933, 2nd ed.)

G. Ebeling, *Theology and Proclamation*, 1966
    (cf. *Theologie und Verkündigung*, 1962)

O. Eissfeldt, *The Old Testament: an Introduction*, 1965
    (cf. *Einleitung in das Alte Testament*, 1964, 3rd ed.)

E. Fuchs, *Studies of the Historical Jesus*, 1964
    (cf. *Ges. Aufsätze*, 1960)

E. Haenchen, *The Acts of the Apostles*, 1971
    (cf. *Die Apostelgeschichte*, 1965, 14th ed.)

F. Hahn, *The Titles of Jesus in Christology*, 1969
    (cf. *Christologische Hoheitstitel*, 1964, 2nd ed.)

M. Hengel, *Judaism and Hellenism*, 1974
    (cf. *Judentum und Hellenismus...*, 1969, 1973²)

J. Jeremias, *Jerusalem in the Time of Jesus*, 1969
    (cf. *Jerusalem zur Zeit Jesu*, 1962, 3rd ed.)
    The Parables of Jesus, 1963
    (cf. *Die Gleichnisse Jesu*, 1965, 7th ed.)
    The Prayers of Jesus, 1967
    (cf. ZNW 35 (1936) (also: *Abba*, 1964)

E. Käsemann, *Essays on New Testament Themes*, 1964
    (cf. *Exegetische Versuche und Besinnungen*, I, 1960)

J. Klausner, *Jesus of Nazareth*, 1929
    (cf. Hebrew original, 1925)

G. Kittel, *Theological Dictionary of the New Testament*, 1964ff.
    (cf. *Theologisches Wörterbuch zum Neuen Testament*, 1932ff.)

W. G. Kümmel, *Promise and Fulfilment*, 1957
    (cf. *Verheissung und Erfüllung*, 1956, 3rd ed.)
    Introduction to the New Testament
    (cf. *Einleitung in das Neue Testament*, 1963, 12th ed.)

G. van der Leeuw, *The Phenomenology of Religion*, 1967
    (cf. *Phänomenologie der Religion*, 1956, 2nd ed.)

R. Otto, *The Kingdom of God and the Son of Man*, 1938
    (cf. *Reich Gottes und Menschensohn*, 1954, 3rd ed.)

H. E. Tödt, *The Son of Man in the Synoptic Tradition*, 1965
    (cf. *Der Menschensohn in der Synoptischen Ueberlieferung*, 1963, 2nd ed.)

E. Schweizer, *Lordship and Discipleship*, 1960
    (cf. *Erniedrigung und Erhöhung bei Jesus und seinen Nachfolgern*, 1955)

A. Schweitzer, *The Quest of the Historical Jesus*, 1954, 3rd ed.
    (cf. *Von Reimarus zu Wrede*, 1906 & c.)

Index

1. Old Testament

2. Old Testament Apochrypha, Pseudepigrapha, Qumran Literature

3. New Testament

4. Rabbinic literature

5. Jewish-Hellenistic literature

6. Greek and Roman writers

7. Early Christian literature

Name Index

Subject Index